My Peace I Leave You

Praise for **My Peace I Leave You**

Having known Kristian Kincaid almost my entire pastoral ministry, I found this book to be everything I could have expected. He is a talented and thoughtful writer. His ability to capture situations and scenarios from his life as a pastor and then make them alive and real for the reader is unparalleled.

Reading this book is like reading through a narration of Luther's Small Catechism. Kincaid's intro stories are captivating and never leave you hanging without resolution. His understanding of the Holy Scriptures reveals a pure Law/Gospel paradigm. The application of justification and sanctification is refreshing.

This book will strengthen the faith life and the vocational life of every reader.

Rev. Dr. Brian Saunders, assistant pastor, Our Redeemer Lutheran Church, Cedar Falls, Iowa; president, Iowa District East of The Lutheran Church—Missouri Synod (LCMS); chairman, LCMS Commission on Theology and Church Relations.

Through the use of modern and biblical stories, Kincaid explores some of the common troubles we Christians face. He doesn't hold back! In vivid language, he discusses the causes and the effects of these troubles.

With the trouble clearly defined, Kincaid then delivers Jesus FOR YOU. The book provides the reader with Scripture passages and prayers to face the troubles of this life in and with the comfort that comes from Jesus Christ and Him alone.

This book can be used devotionally or as a resource for counseling and visitation. The contents could easily be used for a congregational Bible study.

Rev. W. Max Mons, pastor, St. Paul's Lutheran Chapel, Iowa City, Iowa; first vice president, Iowa District East of the LCMS; chairman, board of regents, Concordia Seminary, St. Louis, Missouri.

My Peace I Leave You

CHRIST'S COMFORT IN THE STORMS OF LIFE

KRISTIAN KINCAID

CONCORDIA PUBLISHING HOUSE · SAINT LOUIS

Published by Concordia Publishing House
3558 S. Jefferson Ave., St. Louis, MO 63118–3968
1-800-325-3040 • cph.org

Manufactured in the United States of America

1 2 3 4 5 6 7 8 9 10   34 33 32 31 30 29 28 27 26 25

Contents

Foreword

I have nothing but profound admiration for Kristian Kincaid. He is, for me, a dear friend and a father in the faith. His faithfulness in the office of the ministry and his pastoral care continues to be an example I strive to follow. Kristian simply loves and cares for God's people.

What I admire most about Kristian is that he always gives people hope in Christ. Jesus is there in good times and in bad. Jesus is there from the rising of the sun to its setting. Jesus is there as we live and as we die. At times, this can be difficult to see, but there is never a time when we don't have Jesus. The love of Jesus never falters, never fades, never fails. God is and always will be our refuge and strength, a very present help in every trouble.

Like you, I have faced trouble. Sometimes trouble is caused by the wickedness of others, and sometimes trouble is of my own making. Because we live in fallen world, there is trouble, and when troubles come, it is easy to lose heart. That is where real trouble lies. Trouble has a way of dragging one down into anger and self-pity. Sadly, prayers then falter, God's Word is left unopened, and Christ and His love are forgotten.

Turning away from Christ, distancing oneself from the gifts given through Word and Sacrament, forgetting, questioning, doubting God's love, God's mercy, God's grace—that is troublesome. God is never the problem. We are. Sinfully and foolishly, we let the trouble we face blind us from seeing Jesus and

His love. God forgive us for overlooking Jesus, our greatest help and our only comfort in times of trouble.

It was in my moments of trouble that Kristian's words of encouragement meant the most. He taught me the importance of keeping my head up, of fulfilling my ministry, and of continuing to preach and teach faithfully. He impressed upon me the importance of saying "I'm sorry" not for doctrine but for the sins that we as pastors commit. He showed me the importance of resting my heart on Jesus, of holding the words and promises of Jesus tightly, and of taking comfort in Jesus and His love.

It is that encouragement that I pray finds you in times of trouble. Your problems are no problem for God. The trouble you face is no trouble for Jesus. From the troubled mind that is plagued by godless thoughts, to the troubled heart that has been hardened by sin, to the troubled soul that struggles to see God and His love, Jesus is the answer.

This book is a timely reminder to fix our eyes on Jesus. Jesus sets us free from the trouble of sin, death, and the devil, and Jesus alone can calm our troubled hearts. So, let not your heart be troubled. Jesus is your refuge and strength, a very present help in times of trouble. Pray. Call upon Jesus. For in the day of trouble, He will deliver you. At all times and in all places, rest your heart on Jesus, for Jesus loves you and is and always will be your comfort in times of trouble.

In Christ,

Jesse K. Cearlock, Senior Pastor,
Our Redeemer Lutheran Church, Dubuque, Iowa

Introduction

Life is filled with trouble and trials. There is no way any of us can avoid this fact. A trouble-free life does not exist. Jesus, our compassionate Savior, tells us, "In the world you will have tribulation" (John 16:33). He tells us we will have trouble in this world. It comes from all directions, in all seasons, to all people. It comes to people who do everything right and to those who do everything wrong. It comes because of sin. The fall of mankind brought every imaginable trouble to earth. This source and origination of trouble makes sense, but when we experience it, when we are intimate with it, trouble feels personal.

Far greater than the reality of earthly trouble is the promising truth Jesus speaks in the same verse: "Take heart; I have overcome the world." To take heart is to acknowledge the comforting gifts Christ gives us in His mercy. This is certainly personal.

Take heart. Your life is not defined by trouble or tribulation. Rather, it is defined by Christ and His abiding love for you. He has defeated your trouble, conquered your tribulation.

Take heart. Christ loves you perfectly and profoundly, dearly and deeply, earnestly and eternally. Nothing can separate you from His love. Life in this fallen world is indeed fraught with problems and perplexities, trials and tribulation. This is true. The greater truth is that comfort is richly afforded to us by Christ, our living and loving Savior, through Word and Sacrament.

Take heart; you are never alone or abandoned by Christ. Take heart; His love for you never fades or falters. Never. "Here, weary one," He says, "is My gift of rest for you. Parched one, drink deeply from My refreshing and replenishing cup of love, ever filled to the brim." Take heart; Jesus gives the gift of comfort to the brokenhearted, pardon to the guilt-ridden, peace to the fearful, and abundant and abiding grace to the troubled. Take heart; these comforting gifts that pierce the darkness of every trouble are for you. Every promise of Christ is unbendable and unbreakable. You can join the psalmist in saying, "God is our refuge and strength, a very present help in trouble" (Psalm 46:1).

The world rages, but you need not lose heart by believing there is no hope or help. The world is dark, frightening, and chaotic, but Christ is your comfort and hope at all times and in all circumstances. For your every problem and perplexity, He is the answer. Troubles come; the compassionate Savior never leaves. He is never silenced, aloof, or distant. I readily acknowledge that life is difficult. I have heard it, seen it, and experienced it. You have also. I more eagerly herald the love of Christ for you. The Lord says, "Call upon Me in the day of trouble; I will deliver you, and you shall glorify Me" (Psalm 50:15). The Lord dries your tears and stills your deepest sighs. The Good Shepherd cradles you in His arms and carries you through the deep ravines of trouble and over the steep mountains of tribulation to the lush green pastures and still waters of His love. Take heart. Comfort, hope, peace, and love abound for you from Christ. The Lord delivers on every promise.

Dear reader, what is troubling you?

Trouble comes from within: worry, fear, guilt, despair, and

many others. Trouble comes from without: harsh words, lies, betrayal, unkindness, and actions of others. We face emotional, physical, and spiritual trouble, internal and external trouble, worldly and distant trouble. There's so much turbulence in life. Why is this? Our actions cause trouble for others, and the actions of others cause trouble for us. Daily living involves trials and trouble, problems and perplexities. We are the troubled and the troublers. We have troubled minds, troubled hearts, troubled lives, troubled families. Trouble surrounds us on all sides.

I ask again, what is troubling you? Be honest. Your pillow is stained with tears. Last night, you tossed and turned. Your mind ran a marathon. You can't focus during the day because you are tired and consumed by your thoughts.

A marriage is failing and has proven to be anything but a fairytale. Happily ever after? Who uttered such nonsense? Alas, there is no prince or princess, no happy ending, and no fairy tale.

The phone never rings. The email inbox and the mailbox at your door are empty. You reach out to others, but no one reaches back. Another long, lonely night ensues. Does anyone care?

You upset someone with your words. You spoke first and thought second or third or not at all. Your loose tongue has put you in a tight place. You were hurt when angry words were returned—a dose of your own bitter medicine. The argument remains unsettled, and you play it over and over in your mind. Will this ever be resolved?

A teenage boy is diagnosed with anxiety. He is surrounded by loving parents, caring teachers, capable medical professionals. Yet it takes months to find a medication that works for him. The current medication brings with it side effects that cause him to have suicidal thoughts. Can he survive?

The new hire at work threatens the status quo. He is energetic and has fresh ideas. Other workers seem stale and out of date. He is young. They are old. Older workers expect to be laid off to make room for the next generation. The lines etched on their faces grow deeper as relentless worries about employment take their toll.

A young family is thrilled when their child is born. With joy, they document every milestone. Then symptoms of a disease appear. Trips to the doctor, consultations with specialists, and test after test deliver the devastating news of a rare, rapid, incurable terminal illness. Why would God do this?

You are troubled by the word *family* because yours is fractured. Relationships have been broken for years. You seethe at the mention of your mother. Why haven't you talked to her in all this time? How did this stalemate ever begin? Will it ever end?

A woman driving a car swerved to avoid hitting a deer, but she lost control of her car and hit a tree. Her injuries were severe, and a severed spinal cord left her paralyzed. She will never walk again. What is her purpose now?

Trouble and tribulation are pervasive and persistent. A lost job, a chronic illness, a child with an addiction, a gambling problem, too much alcohol, uncontrollable anger, too much debt, chaos at home, a spouse who has abandoned the faith, a sibling who has rejected Christ, a mental illness.

Fill in the blank honestly: ________________________ troubles me.

Other people seem trouble free. They whistle a merry tune with a spring in every step. They have their act together. But *seem* is the operative word. The statement "I am never troubled" is a troubling lie. The Word of God settles the matter: "Man who is born of a woman is few of days and full of trouble" (Job 14:1). Moses summarizes the span of our days as "toil and trouble" (Psalm 90:10). The sons of Korah collectively state, "My soul is full of troubles" (Psalm 88:3). Our Lord reminds us, "Sufficient for the day is its own trouble" (Matthew 6:34).

Some people are too ashamed to confess their troubles. They gloss over them, change the topic, or even cover them with falsehoods, while others talk only about their problems. Their focus is sharp and narrow on the trouble lurking around every corner. Every sentence is about their own most trying tribulations, their constant concerns.

Itemizing a lengthy list of troubles is not our purpose here. Proclaiming the peace of Christ is!

The Lord is good, a stronghold in the day of trouble; He knows those who take refuge in Him. (Nahum 1:7)

We can speak of peace even in the midst of trials and troubles. In the following pages, we will examine some of the troubles we face in this present day, but—most important—we will concentrate on the one to turn to in every trouble: Jesus Christ. He is our focus. This truth is crystal clear even in the murky darkness: He who silenced the tumultuous and treacherous sea with a word will certainly calm our troubled heart. And then, we will have a trouble-free life, right? No. But will we be comforted in our every trouble? Yes, always. For the one who promises and unfailingly delivers the gifts of peace, comfort, mercy, and hope is Jesus. And He delivers these gifts to us.

Please note that I speak not as a superior to a lesser but as an equal, as one troubled soul to another. No—as one comforted soul to another. This is no lecture from the learned to the unlearned, no tutorial from one untroubled to the hapless troubled. Such foolishness will not surface here. I will not saddle you with directives or formulas for a trouble-free life because no such life exists in this fallen world. The reality is that some situations cannot be resolved. On this side of heaven, some troubles will persist.

Instead, I lovingly point you to Christ—His life, His death, His resurrection, and His gifts of peace and love for you. Our troubles differ, but our comfort is one and the same: Jesus Christ. Let us look to the truths that our Lord gives us in His Word and the gifts of His Holy Supper as we learn together that our lives are not defined by trouble but by the inexhaustible, eternal well of comfort that is Christ and His changeless love for us.

Please, read on. Comfort awaits you in the pages ahead. Peace be with you.

Take heart!

CHAPTER 1

Forgiveness

MY TROUBLE: Guilt

HIS TREASURE: Forgiveness of Sins

TROUBLE: He held his head in his hands. His whole frame shook as he wept, tears so prolific they pooled on the linoleum floor at his feet. This grown man was broken by what he had done. A heavy burden of guilt rested squarely on his shoulders. Slowly and with great effort, the shameful words came, his face still hidden behind trembling fingers. "How can God ever forgive me? Will He forgive me?"

"The blood of Jesus His Son cleanses us from all sin" (1 John 1:7). All. Not some sin; not half—*all. All* is a little word with an enormous impact. This is a tremendous truth for you to treasure. Our heavenly Father did not overlook our sin. He placed the entirety of it on His Son, the Lamb of God, who takes away the sin of the world (see John 1:29). Christ Jesus willingly stretched open His arms to take the entirety and enormity of the world's sin. From the cross, and only from the cross, the blood-soaked Savior cried out, "It is finished" (John 19:30). He completed the work of redeeming us. He paid the price in full; there is no balance due, nothing left for us to do. The wounds of Christ are our healing in full. The death of Christ is our life. His bodily resurrection is proof of our full acquittal. He took our guilt, shame, and sin and gives us the precious gift of forgiveness. We have full pardon. Unearned. Unmerited. Undeserved. The all-knowing Lord forgives and forgets our every sin. He remembers them no more!

But He never forgets you. He is lavish with His forgiveness and does not withhold it for any reason. Ponder this love for you.

We are all poor miserable sinners in thought, word, and deed. This is true and cannot be denied or avoided. We are all by nature sinful and unclean. Sin is not just what we do but what we are. Our Lord states, "For out of the heart come evil thoughts, murder, adultery, sexual immorality, theft, false witness, slander" (Matthew 15:19). We are all filthy rags (see Isaiah 64:6). Sin runs deep—to our very core.

We may try to portray ourselves as squeaky clean, and we fool some people. We may even fool ourselves for a while. But we do not fool the Lord. He knows all about your sin and mine, including the foul secret that resides in the deepest recesses of our hearts. Let's be honest. You are guilty. I am too. We all are. Our every thought, word, and deed is saturated with sin. You cannot undo what you have already done. Neither can I. No one can.

Guilt has relentlessly haunted you and hunted you as prey. Your evasive tactic of being busy gives you respite, but guilt keeps you squarely in the crosshairs. You have attempted to bury your guilt, only to have it resurface in the form of shame. All the excuses you used in the past to explain your behavior ring hollow in the present. Good.

Guilt has its place. We have a God-given conscience that helps us tell the difference between right and wrong, the compass that guides our beliefs and behaviors. This compass makes us uncomfortable, though. It points to our sin. We tend to shield ourselves from discomfort, so we deny our sin. We may become jaded or indifferent or lie to ourselves. If we think we are guiltless, we may no longer care about anything or anyone. What we have done or not done doesn't bother us. "It doesn't really matter what I do," we might tell ourselves. Or we might say, "It is all their fault, not mine!" We become the blameless blamer, deflecting responsibility and defending ourselves, always pointing our finger outward toward others. Deflecting and blaming, deflecting and blaming . . .

To declare ourselves guilt-free is pure callousness and reflects a petrified, hardened heart. We become our own defense lawyer, as well as judge and jury. The trial is quick and easy, and we acquit ourselves. God forbid this verdict, for it jeopardizes our salvation. We should own and confess our sin as David did: "For Your name's sake, O Lord, pardon my guilt, for it is great" (Psalm 25:11). God grant us the gift of sorrow over our own sin. As Paul states, "For godly grief produces a repentance that leads to salvation without regret" (2 Corinthians 7:10).

Speaking of David—when it comes to sin, he thought it, said it, and did it. After his afternoon nap, he rose and casually strolled to a place on the roof. His yawning and stretching were interrupted when he saw a woman bathing on a nearby rooftop. He studied her intensely. Her face. Her figure. Her hair blowing in the breeze. The way the water dripped off her rounded shoulders. She piqued his interest. He studied her more intently, and thoughts of lust became vivid in his mind. He began plotting. The embers of lewdness brightened into raging flames. King David was crowned with his own lust.

He inquired, "Who is this woman?" The answer: Bathsheba, the daughter of Eliam, and the wife of Uriah—one of his own soldiers. Bathsheba stood before David, and he lusted after her. Untroubled David did something most troubling. He committed adultery with Bathsheba. Did he care that Bathsheba was someone else's wife? that her husband was a soldier serving in his army protecting him? Did he care about the Sixth Commandment or what God had said about adultery? David's thoughts, words, and deeds provide the answers.

A knock on the palace door a few weeks later brought news that Bathsheba was pregnant. Pregnant! Now what? David brashly plotted and schemed to make it seem that the infant was Uriah's. "Go home," David told Uriah. "Soldier, spend some time with your dear wife." Dedicated Uriah slept instead at his commander's door. Plan A was foiled. David quickly moved to plan B.

At a meal in Uriah's honor, David kept the drinks flowing until Uriah was drunk. Such a gracious host! "Have another glass. Stumble home and fall into your wife's arms," David urged. Uriah did not go home. Plan B was foiled.

With one sin cascading onto another, David schemed further by ordering Uriah to the warfront, sentencing him to a certain death. This plan worked. An arrow pierced Uriah's flesh, killing him. Untroubled David swept Bathsheba from her rooftop into his arms and put her husband into a dark grave.

Then the Lord sent the prophet Nathan to David. Nathan had a simple story for him. Two men live in a city—one is rich, and one is poor. The poor man has one little ewe lamb, a pet, which lives in the midst of his family. His children play with it, feed it, adore it. All is well and good, until a traveler visits the rich man. Mealtime arrives, and what is there to serve the guest? The poor man's little ewe lamb, nicely roasted and thinly sliced, fits the bill.

David was troubled by the unfairness of the situation. "The rich man deserves to die," David roared. "Who is he? Who is this ruthless man? I will ring his neck!"

Nathan answered, "*You* are the man!" (2 Samuel 12:7, emphasis added). You lusted. You committed adultery. You schemed and plotted. You murdered. You are he!

David finally realized his sin and confessed, "I have sinned against the Lord" (2 Samuel 12:13). These are beautiful words of truth. There were no more excuses, there was no more rationalizing, and there was no more blaming others. David owned his sin.

We should join David in confessing our sin, our own most grievous sin. Our guilty conscience echoes Nathan's words: I am the one. I lied, stole, plotted evil. I committed adultery, lusted, envied, coveted, hated. Shame on me!

No, shame on Jesus.

What? Shame on *Jesus*? Precisely. The Lord has you where He wants you. Not in the crosshairs of damnation but with His cross in full view. He takes our shame and guilt upon Himself. He brings us low so He may raise us up. He breaks us in order to heal us. We take the words of David as our own: "Lord . . . forgive me. I have sinned against You." We see our sinful sickness, and by grace, we behold Jesus, the Great Physician, who absolves our every sin. Why does He do this? Because we have confessed our sin? No. Because of His grace, mercy, and love for us. And because He has already done this—has already died for us, has already reconciled us to our heavenly Father—we confess our sin, our own most grievous sin, known and unknown sins, and lay the whole putrid mess we have made at the pierced feet of Christ. We are guilty—but not guilt-ridden. We are forgiven—purely and profoundly, the most precious gift. We confess with joy, "I believe in . . . the forgiveness of sins" (Apostles' Creed).

Jesus did it all for you. He walked to the cross, each step taken in infinite love. He never wavered to the right or the left. His certain course was the cross. He zealously set His face like flint and carried your sins. Jesus did it. On Calvary, the towering mountain of the world's sin was placed on the strong and sturdy shoulders of Jesus as He willingly hung on the cross. The full weight of our sin and shame is on Jesus. His place was the cross, and He hung there for us, held there by obedient love. He willingly bled, died, and rose for us. "For our sake He made Him to be sin who knew no sin, so that in Him we might become the righteousness of God" (2 Corinthians 5:21). Jesus did it—washing away the mountain of our sin with His rich, red blood. Not a speck remains. Jesus was bound with our sin, and we are set free. Jesus was condemned. We are acquitted.

"Forgiven," every drop of His precious blood unceasingly heralds. "Forgiven," the baptismal font cries out. "Forgiven," our heavenly Father declares. "Forgiven," the Table of the Lord shouts out. Forgiven—full and free! *He* is the man, the flesh-and-blood Savior who loves us. *He* thought it, *He* said it, and

He did it all—for us. Nathan's words to David apply to us also: "The Lord also has put away your sin" (2 Samuel 12:13). The accused are absolved. Take heart. The all-knowing Lord forgives and forgets our every sin. Jesus did it. He is the Savior. Our Savior. What love!

TREASURE: Think back to the beginning of this chapter. What did this man do that made him weep so much? The specific sin is of little importance. What is important is that he considered his sin in the context of the Law of God—the Ten Commandments. What is important is that he was grieved by that sin and repentant for it. What is of paramount importance is what Jesus did and does. His words of love, truth, and absolution are spoken for this man and for us all: "Take heart, My son; your sins are forgiven" (Matthew 9:2).

Take heart, reader. Your sins are forgiven. Even those persistent, seemingly chronic sins that you struggle to overcome. Even when you are confronted daily with the result of your sinful behavior, Jesus forgives you. Jesus bled, died, and rose for you. Go in peace—forgiven, full, and free. The gift of forgiveness is freely given, not just in certain moments but forever. The burden of guilt is lifted. It is such a joy to speak those words of grace to this troubled soul. We have a Savior! Tears of sorrow on this man's cheeks yielded to tears of joy. Full and free forgiveness is the Lord's gift to him. It is also His gift to you.

Jesus has such love for you. Take heart. The gift of full, free forgiveness for *all* of your sin is yours in Christ.

Take Heart

Forgiveness of Sins

The blood of Jesus His Son cleanses us from all sin. (1 John 1:7)

Bless the Lord, O my soul, and forget not all His benefits, who forgives all your iniquity. (Psalm 103:2–3)

I will forgive their iniquity, and I will remember their sin no more. (Jeremiah 31:34)

For I will be merciful toward their iniquities, and I will remember their sins no more. (Hebrews 8:12)

I, I am He who blots your transgressions for My own sake, and I will not remember your sins. (Isaiah 43:25)

Prayer

Lord Jesus Christ, most merciful and loving Savior, I have been sorely troubled by my sin, my own most grievous sin. Guilt weighs heavily upon me. I have sinned against You. Have mercy on me. Grant me the gift of peace, knowing that You zealously went to the cross for me, Your every step taken in pure, boundless love and in willing obedience to Your heavenly Father. Your death is my life. Your wounds are my healing in full. Your precious blood has washed away my every sin. You richly comfort me with what You have done for me as You bled, died, and rose for me and as You declared, "Take heart, My son; your sins are forgiven" (Matthew 9:2). Your pierced hands lifted the heavy burden of guilt from me. My guilty conscience is washed clean by Your holy blood. Thank You for this precious and profound gift. In Your holy name. Amen.

CHAPTER 2

Certainty

MY TROUBLE: Distressing Doubts

HIS TREASURE: Comforting Certainty

TROUBLE: Her questions came in rapid succession: "Does God really love me? How could He after all the things I've done? Is there hope for me? Does He hear my prayers? Does He even care about me?" Her barrage of questions prompts a single query for you: What are the answers for this dear soul?

These feelings of loneliness and despair are familiar. King David asked, "Why are You so far from saving me, from the words of my groaning? O my God, I cry by day, but You do not answer, and by night, but I find no rest" (Psalm 22:1–2). From the cross, Jesus cried out to His Father, "My God, why have You forsaken Me?" (Matthew 27:46). Forsaken! Our blood-soaked Savior suffered alone in agony, in darkness, utterly forsaken by His heavenly Father. They both were in agony. This willing sacrifice was so we would never know such agony, such darkness, such loneliness.

Be assured of this: because of Jesus, you are never separated from God. Sin is the barrier between us and God, but it has already been overcome. We suffer because of sin, not because of God.

Christ, the light of the world, does not leave us to wander in the darkness of doubt, uncertain if we are loved. If He did, then every step here would be taken in absolute dread. Uncertainty is not of God; certainty is. Confusion is not of God; confession is. We have the treasure of God's Holy Word to read, mark for reference, learn from, and take to heart. His Word is our certainty, and on this solid rock, we stand high above the swirling waters of doubt.

We read, "The sum of Your word is truth" (Psalm 119:160). This affords us great and enduring comfort when doubts assail us—and they will. We are not left to grope in the darkness of uncertainty and the deep shadows of doubt, for "Your word is a lamp to my feet and a light to my path" (Psalm 119:105). Our distrustful minds should seek His Word, where He speaks to us, His loved and forgiven children, His heirs of heaven. Case closed. His Word settles the matter. We read, "Every word of God proves true; He is a shield to those who take refuge in Him" (Proverbs 30:5). The stormy sea of doubt is stilled. *Gracious Lord, when the winds and waves of doubt assail me, open my ears to hear Your merciful voice as You speak through Your Holy Word!*

We needlessly put question marks after the Lord's unbreakable promises as the difficulties of our lives give rise to doubts. The Lord declares, "I am with you always" (Matthew 28:20). Period. But we add, "Really, Lord? Because I'm not feeling it right now." "I will remember [your] sins no more" (Hebrews

8:12). Period. Still, we say, "Really?" "For all the promises of God find their Yes in Him" (2 Corinthians 1:20). Period. And again we respond, "Really?" He speaks; we question. He promises; we suspect. We are uncertain about His certain Word.

Impetuous Peter walked on the sea when Jesus bid him to come. But the wind and wave distracted him. The undertow of fear and doubt began to pull him under. Our merciful Lord immediately stretched out His hand and took hold of Peter. Jesus then asked Peter a question that can be addressed to each of us: "O you of little faith, why did you doubt?" (Matthew 14:31). Why do we fear that Jesus will not save us and let the wind pull us into the murky depths of doubt? Isn't the sure and steady hand of Christ always there for us also? It is. Period.

Thomas put a question mark after the wonderful news the other disciples brought him following our Lord's bodily resurrection. "We have seen the Lord," they announced (John 20:25). The living Savior came to them, bestowing the gifts of forgiveness and comfort with His words, "Peace be with you" (John 20:19). He showed them proof of His identity: His pierced hands and the wound in His side where the spear had entered.

Our merciful Lord did not scold or upbraid His fearful disciples on that first Easter evening. Well aware of the dangers they faced, the menace of the very people who had sent Him to His cross, Christ lovingly tended to them with reassurance and peace. He steadied and strengthened them with His Holy Spirit.

Thomas was absent. Where was he? What was he doing? The Bible doesn't tell us. What God tells us is that when he did join them (John 20:24), the other disciples had news: "Thomas," they said, "Jesus lives." They had seen Him for themselves.

The doubtful disciple was not convinced: "Unless I see in His hands the mark of the nails, and place my finger into the mark of the nails, and place my hand into His side, I will never believe" (John 20:25). For Thomas, the light of Easter was still in the dark tomb.

How about you? Even as the Lord speaks a promise in His Word, are you placing a question mark in your present circumstances? Satan badgers us with His incessant lies. "Did God say He loves you? Then why do you have cancer? Then why did your precious baby die? Then why is your husband abusive? Are you sure He loves you? How could He love you and let you lose your job, your parent, your health?" Instead of Satan's odious treachery, you have the treasure trove of God's pure Word. Instead of lies, you have truth. Instead of doubt, we have the declaration of His love. Instead of uncertainty, you have certainty. It is written! Read, mark for reference, learn from, and take to heart all that the Lord says to you in His Word.

Eight long days and nights passed for unbelieving Thomas. What was he doing during that time? What was he thinking? Most important, what would the Lord do with Thomas? Forget him? Chastise him for his weakness in front of the other disciples? Never.

Christ is patient and persistent in His love. The living Lord showed Himself to Thomas, looked directly at him, and spoke to him: "Peace be with you" (John 20:26). The Savior's gift to Thomas was precious peace. His efficacious words provided Thomas with comfort and strength. "My Lord and my God!" Thomas said (v. 28)—not because his eyes saw and his hand touched Jesus but because the love and mercy of the living Savior was poured out for him. Jesus tends to you with the same compassion, just as He tended to Thomas.

Christ speaks to you, dear doubting reader, through His Word and Sacraments. He is never silenced. He comforts and strengthens you, saying, "Peace be with you." He never discards you or tires of tending to you. The light of the world does not leave you in the darkness or leave you to question His love. Rather, He declares His abundant love for you beautifully in His Word, saying, "I have loved you with an everlasting love" (Jeremiah 31:3).

May your doubts drive you to the Word, which drives doubts away. Dark doubts die in the light of God's Word. May you behold the breathtaking truth of His unbreakable promises! Period.

You are weak; Christ is ever strong. You are weary; Christ is ever zealous to refresh and replenish our soul through Word and Sacrament. You are broken; every promise of Christ is unbreakable. Doubts come; Christ stays. Write your name in front of His promises, for they are for you. His love for you is personal. He has carved your name on the palm of His hand, right by the nail print. Take heart! The Lord declares His lavish love for you in His Word, at the font, and in His Holy Supper. Period.

TREASURE: Think back to the beginning of this chapter and the woman I was talking with. Doubts weighed heavily upon her heart and vexed her soul. But there is one place that provides the answers for her and for you—God's Holy Word. As you read that Word, hold His truth in your hands. It is written, and stands written, never to fall or change: God loves you.

This dear soul and I read portions of Psalm 119 together,

and comfort was richly afforded her. "Your word is a lamp to my feet and a light to my path" (v. 105). "The sum of Your word is truth, and every one of Your righteous rules endures forever" (v. 160). "Let my cry come before You, O Lord; give me understanding according to Your word!" (v. 169).

He loves you. This is the Word of the Lord. Thanks be to God! Join her. Opening God's Holy Word slams the lid on doubt. Indeed, doubts wither and die in the light of His Word. Certainty reigns. Thanks be to God. Take heart!

Take Heart

Comforting Certainty

Sanctify them in the truth; Your word is truth. (John 17:17)

A bruised reed He will not break, and a faintly burning wick He will not quench. (Isaiah 42:3)

I am severely afflicted; give me life, O Lord, according to Your word! (Psalm 119:107)

I believe; help my unbelief! (Mark 9:24)

Peace I leave with you; My peace I give to you. Not as the world gives do I give to you. Let not your hearts be troubled, neither let them be afraid. (John 14:27)

Prayer

Gracious Lord, Your Word is truth. Comfort and certainty flow forth as I read Your inspired and inerrant Word. I am weak, but Your Word is my strength. I doubt, but Your Word assures me. Your voice of mercy and love is sweeter than honey and more precious than gold. Your Word is nourishment and sustenance for my weary soul. I rejoice, for "Your Word is truth" and my comfort in all situations and at all times. In Jesus' name. Amen.

CHAPTER 3

Facing Difficulties

MY TROUBLE: Discouraged by Difficulty

HIS TREASURE: Strength to Endure Difficulty

TROUBLE: After nearly fifty years in the workforce, a woman joined her husband in retirement. Together, they had raised a family, celebrated the births of their grandchildren, bought and paid for a home, saved a portion of their earnings, and made travel plans. Their friends and relatives rejoiced with them and wished them well.

Then the husband suffered a debilitating stroke. At first, it wasn't certain if he would live. His wife and everyone who knew the couple prayed for strength and courage, for hope and the assurance of Christ's mercy.

Her husband lived, but the damage was severe. He could no longer walk or feed himself. The couple had inadequate insurance to pay for long-term care and therapy; this only added to the tragedy. The only option was for him to return home. Their savings were used to pay for a ramp to the house and a chairlift to navigate the stairs to the bedroom. The man's wife, who had vowed to care for her husband "in sickness and in health" and "for better, for worse" (*LSB*, p. 276), stayed by his side through it all. But the couple experienced deep depression and grief due to what they had lost. It wasn't supposed to be like this.

How do you handle difficulties that arise in your life? Do you face them or retreat from them? Difficulties come in various forms to each of us. What are the difficulties in your life? Although your difficulty may not be as weighty as a stroke that takes away your ability to walk, any difficulty poses challenges. Do difficulties discourage you? You cannot change the circumstances of your life, but your loving Lord can certainly change your heart. Therefore, your approach and attitude toward life is affected. Difficulties certainly will come, and the ensuing discouragement they can bring may cause you to mutter, "There is no way through this." That's when you needlessly forfeit the strength the Lord affords you, the fortitude to face and endure difficulties of any magnitude.

Your gracious Savior bids you to cast any and every difficulty upon Him. He hears your every prayer. Discouragement is therefore replaced with, "Lord, encourage and strengthen me." He will. Paul wrote, "For whatever was written in former days was written for our instruction, that through endurance and through the encouragement of the Scriptures we might have hope" (Romans 15:4). The Bible is filled with example after example of God-given endurance and encouragement.

Think of Moses. The Lord told him, "I will send you to Pharaoh that you may bring My people, the children of Israel, out of Egypt" (Exodus 3:10). Moses was discouraged. He stated, "Who am I that I should go?" (Exodus 3:11). He said the people would not believe him (Exodus 4:1), that he was not eloquent, and that he was slow of speech (Exodus 4:10). Discouraged, Moses muttered, "This is too difficult."

Think of Elijah. The prophet declared that he was done. He was discouraged that Queen Jezebel sought to kill him. Under a broom tree, he lamented, "It is enough; now, O Lord, take away my life, for I am no better than my fathers" (1 Kings 19:4). Dejected, Elijah said, "I can't do this anymore."

Think of Jeremiah. The Lord called him as a prophet to the nations, alerting them to the coming destruction because they had turned away from God. Dismayed, Jeremiah said, "I do not know how to speak, for I am only a youth" (Jeremiah 1:6).

The Lord calls us, too, to witness to our faith in Him even when the world has rejected Him. He says to us, "Fear not, for I am with you; be not dismayed, for I am your God; I will strengthen you, I will help you, I will uphold you with My righteous right hand" (Isaiah 41:10). Note the five times "I" is stated in the verse and the gifts the Lord gives us. Our gracious Lord also "gives power to the faint, and to him who has no might He increases strength" (Isaiah 40:29).

Moses was saved from slavery. Emboldened by the Lord, he spoke to Pharaoh and prophesied the ten warnings (the plagues); then he led the people across the divided Red Sea. Moses and the children of Israel stood safely on the opposite shore and lifted their voices to sing, "The Lord is my strength and my song, and He has become my salvation; this is my God, and I will praise Him" (Exodus 15:2). Promise kept. Strength given.

Elijah did not die under the broom tree. The Lord strengthened him to stand, speak boldly, live, and move forward. There is little wonder that Elisha asked for a double portion of Elijah's spirit before Elijah was taken to heaven in a whirlwind (see 2 Kings 2:9).

Youthful Jeremiah was rescued from the muddy pit and directed by God to share words of warning and love to people who rejected him. He said of God, "You came near when I called on You; You said, 'Do not fear!'" (Lamentations 3:57).

The Lord strengthened Samson to face a lion, David to face Goliath, and Daniel to face a den of lions. He strengthened Shadrach, Meshach, and Abednego to go into a blazing furnace. He strengthened Stephen to pray, even as he was stoned to death. He strengthened Paul to endure shipwrecks, beatings, riots, sleepless nights, hunger, and imprisonment. The Lord strengthened others to endure the difficulties of being mocked, tortured, stoned, and imprisoned (see Hebrews 11).

We understand that Paul would speak of despair and burdens (see 2 Corinthians 1:8). But then the apostle wrote, "For the sake of Christ, then, I am content with weaknesses, insults, hardships, persecutions, and calamities. For when I am weak, then I am strong" (2 Corinthians 12:10).

Our greatest comfort in the midst of difficulties is Jesus, our Lord, who set His face like flint to the cross. Christ willingly faced the most extreme difficulties of body and soul that would ever be—all for our sake. We should "consider Him who endured from sinners such hostility against Himself, so that you do not grow weary or fainthearted" (Hebrews 12:3). Jesus was betrayed and rejected by His own followers. A man of sorrows, He was despised, wounded, crushed, stricken, smitten, afflicted, crushed by His contemporaries. It got worse: Jesus was forsaken by His Father, oppressed, cut off from the living (see

Isaiah 53). His appearance was marred beyond human semblance (see Isaiah 52). He was whipped, beaten, slapped, and spat upon to the extent that He was one bloody wound that hung from the cross. Such travail and anguish of body and soul is beyond our comprehension. He was oppressed and afflicted, yet "He opened not His mouth" (Isaiah 53:7). He did not beckon an angel to wipe His bloody brow. Through parched lips and raging thirst, our Lord prayed, "Father, into Your hands I commit My spirit!" (Luke 23:46). Such difficulty. Such suffering. Such love.

Consider this: Christ loves you all the way to the cross and empty tomb. He endured all this travail of body and soul for you. The living one is with you. He hears your every prayer. You face nothing alone, for "the eyes of the LORD are toward the righteous" (Psalm 34:15). Despite the most difficult circumstances the world can put you in, no matter what you may face, there is no reason for you to grow weary, fainthearted, or discouraged. Amidst the changing scenes and circumstances of your life, Jesus' love and compassion for you is unchanging. With the faith given to you by the Holy Spirit, you can boldly say,

> **For I am sure that neither death nor life, nor angels nor rulers, nor things present nor things to come, nor powers, nor height nor depth, nor anything else in all creation, will be able to separate us from the love of God in Christ Jesus our Lord. (Romans 8:38–39)**

Do difficulties surround you? Are you discouraged? Me too. Let us turn to the Word of the Lord:

My soul melts away for sorrow; strengthen me according to Your Word!" (Psalm 119:28)

This is my comfort in my affliction, that your promise gives me life. (Psalm 119:50)

He gives power to the faint, and to Him who has no might, He increases strength. (Isaiah 40:29)

We can read, mark for reference, learn from, and take to heart all that the living Word bestows. Comfort and strength abound. Therefore, "we are afflicted in every way, but not crushed; perplexed, but not driven to despair; persecuted, but not forsaken; struck down, but not destroyed" (2 Corinthians 4:8–9).

Difficulties? Pray without ceasing (see 1 Thessalonians 5:17). "On the day I called, You answered me; my strength of soul You increased" (Psalm 138:3). Turn to the Lord with all your difficulties. You can say, "But truly God has listened; He has attended to the voice of my prayer" (Psalm 66:19). The Lord's love opens your lips to declare, "On the day I called, You answered me; my strength of soul You increased."

Difficulties? Remember your Baptism. By grace, you are God's dear child, blood-bought and redeemed, washed in His blood, robed in His righteousness, an heir of heaven. "I am baptized" are three powerful and encouraging words to remember at all times. Make use of your Baptism daily to drown the pessimistic old Adam so that the new Adam comes forth. Cherish the gifts of faith, forgiveness, and eternal life given to you by God at the baptismal font. Treasure this truth daily: "For as many of you as were baptized into Christ have put on

Christ" (Galatians 3:27). You, a beloved child of God, robed in His righteousness, and ready to face all that lies ahead.

Difficulties? Weekly walk through the doors of the Lord's house. The Lord gives precious gifts to you in the Divine Service. Remember—one day here is better than a thousand elsewhere (see Psalm 84:10). Hear and treasure the words of Holy Absolution as from Christ Himself. Hear the proclamation of Christ and His love from the pulpit. The Bread of Life feeds you at His Table. Receive His body and blood in, with, and under the bread and wine for the forgiveness of your sins and the strengthening of Your faith. You leave the Lord's house spiritually fed, nourished, comforted, and strengthened, ready to enter daily life hearing, as Joshua did, "Be strong and courageous. Do not be frightened, and do not be dismayed, for the LORD your God is with you wherever you go" (Joshua 1:9).

TREASURE: Recall the woman at the beginning of this chapter whose retirement years were irrevocably changed after her husband had a stroke. She was physically and mentally exhausted by the daily and nightly care her husband required. She grew weary trying to keep his spirits up and remain cheerful in the face of his frustration and sadness. Some days, when the heartbreaking, backbreaking work of caring for him threatened to take her last shred of joy, all she had was memorized words of Scripture to see her through.

The husband, too, felt the tremendous weight of frailty of human flesh. His body could not do what he needed it to do, and his mind was burdened by sadness, guilt, and anger. What was his purpose now? He was nothing more than a burden to his wife. He begged God to let him die.

Too tired, too discouraged to pray, this couple faced their tribulation with the help of the Holy Spirit, who prays for us when we cannot. Their faith, which was given to them in Baptism, assured them of healing and wholeness by our compassionate Christ. And they knew that this terrible time would end. Their days on earth are numbered. Their inheritance was earned by the work of Jesus on the cross.

> **In this you rejoice, though now for a little while, if necessary, you have been grieved by various trials, so that the tested genuineness of your faith—more precious than gold that perishes though it is tested by fire—may be found to result in praise and glory and honor at the revelation of Jesus Christ. Though you have not seen Him, you love Him. Though you do not now see Him, you believe in Him and rejoice with joy that is inexpressible and filled with glory, obtaining the outcome of your faith, the salvation of your souls. (1 Peter 1:6–9)**

Take Heart

Strength to Endure Difficulty

It is the LORD who goes before you. He will be with you; He will not leave you or forsake you. Do not fear or be dismayed. (Deuteronomy 31:8)

May the God of hope fill you with all joy and peace in believing, so that by the power of the Holy Spirit you may abound in hope. (Romans 15:13)

Be strong, and let your heart take courage, all you who wait for the LORD! (Psalm 31:24)

For I, the LORD your God, hold your right hand; it is I who say to you, "Fear not, I am the one who helps you." (Isaiah 41:13)

Though he fall, he shall not be cast headlong, for the LORD upholds his hand. (Psalm 37:24)

Prayer

Gracious Lord, I turn to You for hope and strength in the midst of this difficulty. I am never alone, for You, who bled, died, and rose, will never leave me or forsake me. Your unchanging love is my constant comfort. I turn to You in my weakness, for You are my strength. I am sorely afflicted. Give me life according to Your Word. In Jesus' name. Amen.

CHAPTER 4

Fearfully and Wonderfully Made

MY TROUBLE: **Pride, Self-Loathing**

HIS TREASURE: **You—Fearfully and Wonderfully Made**

TROUBLE: I noticed the bruises on her face right away. Makeup concealed most of them, but under her left eye, discolorations were clearly evident. It was a teenager who obviously and sadly was in someone's line of abusive fire.

You are fearfully and wonderfully made, knit together in your mother's womb by the Creator, skillfully and masterfully designed. This is true of every human being without exception. This is a humbling and profound truth that led David to write, "I praise You, for I am fearfully and wonderfully made" (Psalm 139:14). We are all uniquely made by the Lord. There is no one else like you in the entire universe, nor will there ever be. As Job said, "Did not He who made me in the womb make him? And did not one fashion us in the womb?" (Job 31:15). Certainly so!

The Lord wove together your inward parts (Psalm 139:13). He fashioned your organs and masterfully knit you together as bone, sinew, and flesh. Think about that for a moment. If you are not amazed at this, then I ask you, do you know how many hairs the Lord has placed on your head? Do you know how many millions of rods and cones are in your eyes? Do you know how many thousands of miles of blood vessels are in your body? I beg you to research these questions! There are many more astounding facts about your body attesting to the truth that you are indeed wonderfully made. Wonderful are His works! There is no room for pride or negativity when we rightly focus on the truth that God created us.

In light of the truth that the Creator knit you together, how do you fill in the blank to this statement: "I am ____________________." What words would you use to describe yourself? Positive or negative? Rooted in fact or fiction? Scripturally or societally based? We often like to compare ourselves to others and then look down upon them from the self-erected scaffolding of pride. We realize that we may not be the best, but we certainly are a rung or two higher than others on the ladder of importance. There is always a predetermined winner and loser as we live this way. Everything becomes a competition. We read, "By insolence comes nothing but strife" (Proverbs 13:10). Who wants to be saddled with someone who thinks he or she is better than everyone else and says so? What kind of relative or friend would that be? (Have you ever wondered if this person is you?)

The scaffolding of pride is a shaky place to stand. In fact, looking down on others is the lowest vantage point!

But our pride contends that we are the best. According to whom? According to me, myself, and I. The smartest? Me. The hardest worker? Me. The strongest faith. Me. Who can be compared to me? No one! This is delusion of self by grandeur. Pride is to worship the idol of self.

A great fault is to be aware of none of our own. I stood in a Nebraska wheat field years ago with an elderly farmer. One of his younger neighbors joined us and belittled the older man's wheat crop, saying his own field was bigger, better, and would certainly be more productive and lucrative. The boastful neighbor stood with head high, on his tiptoes, arm outstretched pointing to his own wheat field across the road. "See how high my wheat is," he boasted. "Do you see my field of grain?" the older man softly said. "Only the empty heads of grain stand tall."

Empty statements: "I make the most money." "I am the most generous." "I am the most athletic." "I have the best figure." "I was named most likely to succeed." "I was the homecoming queen." "I am better looking than you." "I am richer than you." "I am smarter than you."

What self-important thoughts do you have? What boastful statements have come from your lips? More important—why? Who are you trying to impress? Why are you so concerned with what others think of you? Why stand so tall—and yet so empty? "The empty ones stand the tallest . . ."

Conceit and boastfulness can be equated with lies that we tell ourselves. Such as, "I am better than everybody else, more important than anyone else, more deserving than everyone else." This is "I" trouble of the worst sort, where we magnify our influence and importance. We can live this way and, sadly, die this way. Yet my gravestone will be larger than yours, my obituary will be lengthy and full of my accomplishments. Live tall, die tall. Comparing and competing unto death. "The empty ones stand the tallest . . ."

We all have strengths and weaknesses. Better yet is to know that the Lord created all of us. Better above all is for us to ponder the humility of Christ. The Creator deigns to be with His creation, humbly taking on our flesh for our sake. The omnipotent One is carried in the confines of Mary's womb, is born in a stable, and is laid in a manger. There is no feather bed, castle, or fortress for Christ. There is love. There is a cross. Christ "humbled Himself by becoming obedient to the point of death, even death on a cross" (Philippians 2:8).

"O Lord, open my lips . . ." How does that verse end? "O Lord, open my lips, and my mouth will declare *my* praises." No. "O Lord, open my lips, and my mouth will declare *Your* praises" (Psalm 51:15, emphasis added). To speak of Christ is far better than to speak of yourself. To build others up in love is far better than to build yourself up in ugly arrogance.

The opposite of exalting oneself is self-loathing, like when we mutter, "Everyone is better than me." "I am worthless." "I am ugly." "I am stupid." "I am a mistake." Have you thought such lies about yourself? Is the parasite of worthlessness constantly gnawing on your heart and mind? Why? Because someone in your life said you were less than them. Maybe a parent, classmate, teacher, employer, coach, or spouse said you were inadequate. Someone said you were homely. Someone said you were not as smart as your sibling. Someone said you were an embarrassment, would never amount to anything, were worthless. Someone said you were fat. Someone said you don't fit in with popular groups, you don't belong. Someone said they were ashamed of you, no one would ever love you . . .

A student I had in confirmation class some years ago excelled with memory work and exams. Smart kid! His work, however, began to slip after a few months. Superior work slipped to inferior. He didn't raise his head or hand in class anymore and grew increasingly quiet. He stopped talking to other students. I asked if everything was all right. He tersely replied, "Yes," without looking at me. I didn't believe him.

I decided to stop by his home on a Saturday morning to check in with him. As I walked up to the front door, I heard screaming. "You idiot," a woman yelled. "You piece of worthless ______. I wish you had never been born. Get the ____ out of my sight." I no longer wondered what the problem was.

I rang the doorbell and waited. The door opened after a few moments. "Good morning," the mother politely said, her tone drastically different from what I had overheard just moments before. "Come in." The student I had come to visit was curled up on the sofa weeping. "He's having a bad day. Say good morning to the pastor," she ordered. This was no good morning.

Who says to a child, "You idiot. I wish you had never been born"? Who levels the charge, "You are nothing!" There is no excuse to treat anyone this way—ever. Who does such great harm? Damaged people who then damage others. Some of us have been deeply wounded and badly damaged. Words cut deep and leave unseen scars. Abusive actions often leave literal marks. The ghastly voice of abuse is heard in our minds over and over.

Jesus heard the most damaging of words: "Crucify Him!

We don't want Him. We don't believe in Him. We reject Him!" Jesus understands the pain inflicted by such words and comforts and consoles the hurting. His truth expels and triumphs over the repulsive lies of others.

Jesus beautifully said you are precious in His sight, you are His own dear child.

"You clothed me with skin and flesh, and knit me together with bones and sinews" (Job 10:11). These words are true of every human being. This is not the emptiness of self-esteem but the fullness of scriptural truth—a humbling truth! What we say of ourselves is one thing. What God says of us is another.

Listen: "Did not He who made me in the womb make him? And did not one fashion us in the womb?" (Job 31:15). We are all fashioned and created by the Lord.

Listen: "Before I formed you in the womb I knew you" (Jeremiah 1:5). We are all formed and fashioned by the Lord.

You are a precious child of God. Baptized, blood-bought, redeemed, an heir of heaven. That covers it. No need to boast. No need to wallow in self-pity. You are His. The Lord created you and redeemed you, all in the most lavish of love. He short-changes no one. He has gifted you. You are unique, as your fingerprints and the pupils in your eyes attest. God said, "You are my precious child. I made you. I chose you. I redeemed you by the blood of My Son." Take heart!

Are you wondering about that confirmand? I talked with him before and after each class and encouraged him with the truth of Christ and His love. A year later, he was confirmed. He chose Psalm 139:14 as his confirmation verse: "I praise You, for I am fearfully and wonderfully made." I wish you could have seen his smile as he shook my hand after the service.

TREASURE: Think back to the young woman I described at the beginning of this chapter. Those bruises on her face. It was clear that something terrible had happened. "Please, tell me," I said. "What happened? Who did this to you?" The sad truth is that she had done it to herself. This pattern of self-harm had been going on for years—since middle school. Invisible wounds deep inside her led to visible wounds on her. She was fat, the popular girls said, adding even more damaging words: chunky, ugly, slow, lardo, a waste of space. Unkind words and laughter gave way to open and foul ridicule every day. How deep the wounds. "They're right," she said. "I am ugly." She loathed what she saw in the mirror.

Why did she internalize these foul lies about herself? Why do you? What God says is truth, and you can rest your heart on His Word. He created you, masterfully and wonderfully. The Lord Himself declares that you are His handiwork.

This young woman and I spoke many times during her high school years, focusing on what the Lord said about her. She put a note on her mirror: "Created and redeemed by Christ." Her family sought counseling for her, a wise and loving move from concerned parents. Her inner narrative began to change. Thanks be to God!

As often happens, people drift in and out of our lives. This young woman and her family moved away. When I see her photo in an old church directory, I pray that life has been kind to her over the two decades that have passed. I pray that she has been kind to herself. I pray that she has hung on to the truth that she is "fearfully and wonderfully made." I pray that you hang on to that truth too.

Take Heart

You—Fearfully and Wonderfully Made

You clothed me with skin and flesh, and knit me together with bones and sinews. You have granted me life and steadfast love, and Your care has preserved my spirit. (Job 10:11–12)

Thus says the LORD, your Redeemer, who formed you from the womb: "I am the LORD, who made all things, who alone stretched out the heavens, who spread out the earth by Myself." (Isaiah 44:24)

But now, O LORD, You are our father; we are the clay, and You are our potter; we are all the work of Your hand. (Isaiah 64:8)

My frame was not hidden from You, when I was made in secret, intricately woven in the depths of the earth. (Psalm 139:15)

Know that the LORD, He is God! It is He who made us, and we are His; we are His people, and the sheep of His pasture. (Psalm 100:3)

Prayer

Gracious and merciful Father, thank You for creating me. You knit me together miraculously and masterfully. I am not an accident but Your own handiwork, fearfully and wonderfully made. My life is a gift from You. Forgive me for my sinful pride and for needlessly demeaning myself. Thank You for redeeming me with the precious blood of Your dear Son. Thank You for re-creating me in Holy Baptism, where You washed my sin-stained heart and bestowed on me the gifts of faith, forgiveness, and eternal life. I have peace knowing that I am your child, loved, forgiven, and redeemed. Help me encourage others with these tremendous truths. In Jesus' name. Amen.

CHAPTER 5

Peace

MY TROUBLE: Worry (No, Worries)

HIS TREASURE: Peace

TROUBLE: It was a hot and humid July day in Iowa with an excessive heat warning issued. Corn flourishes under these conditions; human beings not so much. The city tennis tournament was still on, despite the dangerous weather. Our college-age son participated in the tournament from early morning to late afternoon.

Walking across the street at noon to our mailbox was oppressive for me. With beads of sweat on my brow, I thought of my son. It was odd that we hadn't heard from him. How did his doubles match go in these conditions?

My wife and I decided to drive to the meet and find out. When we got there, nearly everyone had left. The only ones remaining were our son and a couple of his friends, who stood on the parking lot.

"I don't think he should drive home," his doubles partner

said. “He seems confused.”

He was. In less than an hour, our son was in a hospital emergency room. Heat exhaustion was worrisome enough. Then things got worse—he had two severe seizures. Hours later, our son was flown to Madison, Wisconsin, on a Life Flight helicopter. *Life Flight*. Let those terrifying words sink in.

Our two-hour drive to Madison was excruciating for us physically, mentally, and spiritually. We did not know if our son was dead or alive. Our hearts were in pieces. Dread and worry . . . every inch and every second of that drive . . . *dread and worry . . . dread and worry . . . Life Flight . . . dread and worry.*

Jesus Christ is the Prince of Peace. “On earth peace among those with whom He is pleased,” the angelic host joyously proclaimed at His birth (Luke 2:14). The manger held the flesh-and-blood Savior—peace on earth literally! The loving Prince of Peace willingly suffered travail of body and turbulence of soul for our sake. The depth of His suffering reveals the towering height of His love for us. His holy face never looked away from Calvary. He was unfairly accused and judged, slapped, spit upon, ridiculed, mocked, stripped, and flogged. Our condemned Christ took our place on the cross willingly and lovingly. He hung suspended between heaven and earth, His holy arms fully open to take the sin of world and the wrath of His Father.

Travail of body and soul. There was no peace for the Prince of Peace as wood and nails awaited Him. Yet there *is* peace for you from the living Savior. Jesus teaches about the heavenly Father’s lavish care for you in a lesson focusing on birds and lilies, of all things. What do birds and flowers have to do with me and my worries, you ask? The answer is in the comforting truth that Christ teaches.

Did you know that the Lord created as many as eleven thousand species of birds? Astonishing. They vary in size, color, wingspan, beak size, diet, type of nest, and location. The Lord knows the actual number and, more astonishingly, not one bird falls to the ground without His knowledge. Worry does not rob a bird of its song or its next meal.

Did you know that there are more than two thousand varieties of lilies? One can speak of the royal lily, the martagon lily, and the asiflorum lily. Their colors vary from white, pink, yellow, red, and orange. Such beautiful hues the Lord has painted these delicate blossoms! What do lilies have to do with my worries? Not one of these plants toils or spins. The Lord simply takes care of them, sending sunshine and showers. That's the beauty of the Creator's care!

Did you know that the average human head has 100,000 hairs? Did you know that the blood vessels in your body laid end to end would stretch on average 62,000 miles? Did you know that there are 60 million cones and 120 rods in your eyes? These are astonishing truths about you. In fact, the greatest wonder on earth is *you*.

Did you know that the Creator takes care of you? His providence and care cannot be exhausted. The Bread of Life provides daily bread for you, along with a cornucopia of other gifts. Every breath, every heartbeat are His gifts to you. He never tires of providing for you. Everything comes with a little gift tag reading, "From your heavenly Father—with love." He will tirelessly and faithfully take care of you, abundantly blessing you with all the love, forgiveness, grace, mercy, and peace you could possibly need. Daily bread. Not weekly, monthly, or yearly—daily. "Do not worry," Jesus bids us. "I am not aloof or distant. I am with you always, and I care for you always. Every single day without exception, I offer you abundant gifts."

We need not fret or worry, for what good does worry do? It changes nothing. Birds do not worry. Lilies do not worry. Yet we, the crown of His creation, worry. Unnecessarily so. "Right now, what worries me is ______________________." We worry about the past, the present, and the future. We fret, even though we know that the Lord holds these times and each of us in His loving hands. As we worry, we toss contradictory thoughts around in our minds such as these: *There is hope. There is no hope. I will get through this. I will never get through this. This will turn out all right. This will end in disaster.*

Worry adds to our stress and subtracts from life. Worry suffocates and squeezes the joy out of today, tonight, and tomorrow. Worry robs us of enjoying the present moment and subsequent moments. The origin of the word *worry* means "to strangle." Worry suffocates, strangles, and squeezes the breath out of hope. (Is that you I hear gasping?)

We worry about things that will never happen and about things that have happened. We worry during the day and at night. We worry about our family, our employment, our finances. We worry about what others think of us. Worry takes the Lord out of the equation and makes Him aloof, distant, uncaring. (Nothing could be further from the truth!)

"Don't worry about it," others glibly tell us, which only makes us worry more. The hands of worry squeeze our necks a little tighter. It's hard to breathe, isn't it? Today we worry, tonight we worry, tomorrow we worry. Worrisome thoughts invade our minds: *What shall we eat? What shall we drink? What shall we wear? What shall we do?* You are anxious and troubled over many things when all you need to do is listen to Christ. Be still and know that He is the Lord. Take a deep breath.

Listen. Jesus addresses our every worry with His love. He bids us to consider the birds of the air (Matthew 6:25–34). Not one of the many species of birds God created sows or reaps or gathers into barns. The birds sing without worry. Their songs are heard before the first streaks of light appear in the morning and continue until the last rays depart at dusk. Some even continue through the night. They sing when the sky is blue and when it is gray. They are not robbed of their song by worry. The psalmist writes, "They sing among the branches" (Psalm 104:12). This is a theological lesson, not a biological one.

God takes care of every single bird. Not one bird ever falls to the ground without His knowledge. The Lord says, "I know all the birds of the hills, and all that moves in the field is Mine" (Psalm 50:11). How much more zealously will He take care of you, His precious child! When was the last time you considered the value of a bird? Are you more precious than any bird? Yes! Would He watch over a bird and take His merciful eyes off you? Never. Worry is needless and useless! You need not let worry rob you of your song, for "He put a new song in my mouth, a song of praise to our God" (Psalm 40:3).

Our Lord inquires, "Which of you by being anxious can add a single hour to his span of life?" (Luke 12:25). Worry is hard on our bodies and minds. Worry does not add the tiniest fraction of time to our lives. The opposite is true. Worry subtracts from the quality and quantity of our lives and adds nothing but wrinkles on our faces and anxious minds and hearts. Worry opposes the Lord's care and providence for us as it makes us think the Lord is aloof and uncaring.

Listen. Jesus bids us also to consider the lilies of the field. Pause from your business of worry and ponder these flowers. See them blowing in the breeze. Consider how they grow and that they neither toil nor spin. See them basking in the sunshine. See them as the rain falls upon the soil. The Lord takes care of them. The point is not the beauty of the flower petals. Beautiful though they are, the true beauty is that of the Lord's constant care and provision for each bloom on every plant. Even more so, the point is that the Lord cares for and provides for each of us. Worrying is needless and useless!

So then, how do we live? To be told to stop worrying is a bothersome and unachievable directive. It's easier said than put into practice. Better is to know that, when we worry—and we certainly will—we can turn to Christ. He will provide for us. He is calm during the tempest. He is our rock and refuge. He is our peace when our hearts are torn in pieces by worry. He bestows the gift of peace in the midst of the most worrisome storms. Great at times are our worries. Greater at all times is the love of the Savior. Christ provides us with comfort. Continually. Daily. Unfailingly. Always.

Take heart. Christ attends to us most lovingly, constantly, without fail or interruption. We live amidst stress and strain, tribulation and turmoil, loss and grief. There is little wonder that our hearts and minds race! Yet not one hair of our head falls to the ground without the Lord's knowledge. He is our peace amid every storm. He has unlimited strength to bear our worries. "Cast your burden on the Lord, and He will sustain you" (Psalm 55:22). We can cast our burden on Christ whenever it arises, no matter what. Not one concern of ours is too trivial or too cumbersome for Him. Paul reminds us, "My God will supply all every need of yours according to His riches in glory in Christ Jesus" (Philippians 4:19). This is a most comforting truth. We are not robbed of our song but can join the psalmist in saying, "He put a new song in my mouth, a song of praise to our God" (Psalm 40:3). The Lord is good to us always. Take heart!

Please go outside, take a deep breath, sit, listen, look, and learn lessons the Lord teaches you through the birds and flowers.

TREASURE: Our son on a Life Flight. Our son in an intensive care unit. Heat stroke, seizures, induced coma. Our minds recoiled at the unfamiliar scene of tubes and noisy machines; at strange faces in the neurology unit speaking medical jargon. The impersonal hospital hallways fueled our uncertainty. Would he live? Would he suffer brain damage? Were his plans for the future destroyed? *Dread and worry.* "O Lord, have mercy."

We turned to Christ, knowing He was with us and that He loved our son even more than we could. Faithful pastors and friends pointed us to Christ and prayed for us and our son. You have stood there, too, haven't you? In difficult places and situations where your heart pounded with worry and your mind raced with fear. We go to Christ and Christ alone for comfort, peace, and hope, even in the midst of the most dreadful situations.

Our compassionate Lord heard our prayers and responded with healing. Our son would be fine and was released from the hospital after a few days. There was no lasting damage from the heat stroke and seizures. He could proceed with his plans for a career in the medical field. God's hand of mercy is clearly seen. If we had not taken him to the emergency room when we did, if Life Flight had not gotten him to the intensive care unit in a matter of minutes, our son would not be with us today. Thanks be to God the seizures took place in the hospital. My wife's phone had 1 percent battery left when she called the doctor who implored, "Take him in *now*." Coincidences? No.

The drive home with him from Madison was wonderful. We savored every inch and second of the trip. God's loving hand holds us all—always.

Take Heart

Peace

Fear not, for I am with you; be not dismayed, for I am your God; I will strengthen you, I will help you, I will uphold you with My righteous right hand. (Isaiah 41:10)

Cast your burden on the LORD, and He will sustain you; He will never permit the righteous to be moved. (Psalm 55:22)

Therefore I tell you, do not be anxious about your life. (Matthew 6:25)

Humble yourselves, therefore, under the mighty hand of God so that at the proper time He may exalt you, casting all your anxieties on Him, because He cares for you. (1 Peter 5:6–7)

Do not be anxious about anything, but in everything by prayer and supplication with thanksgiving let your requests be made known to God. And the peace of God, which surpasses all understanding, will guard your hearts and minds through Christ Jesus. (Philippians 4:6–7)

Prayer

Gracious Lord, I have been worried and troubled over so many things, which separates me from You and wrongly makes You seem distant and uncaring. Forgive me. May I remember to cast the burden of my worries on You and receive from You the gift of peace that passes all human understanding. You still my racing mind and trembling heart. You provide sustenance for my body and nourishment for my soul unfailingly. Your love and care for me knows no end. Open my lips to speak of the wonders of Your love and not words of needless worry. In Jesus' name. Amen.

CHAPTER 6

The Living Word

MY TROUBLE: Words Spoken and Heard

HIS TREASURE: His Holy Word

TROUBLE: Harsh words had been spoken between a father and son years before. "I hate you!" the son yelled. "I wish you had never been born!" the father screamed back. He added salt to the wound with, "Get out of here! I never want to see you again. *Get out!*" An uppercut here, a jab there, another sucker punch. It was a boxing match with words, each one seeking a knockout. The silence between them lasted a decade. All attempts to reconcile by one or the other proved futile. What we say, what we don't say, our facial expressions, our body language, and our tone of voice reveals what resides in the deep recesses of our heart.

The father and son lived only thirty miles apart, but the emotional distance was immeasurable. Flash forward to the present: a hospital room where the dad is dying of cancer and is expected to live only a few more hours. What matters now?

Being right? Winning an argument? Putting someone in his place? Lost time is never found.

I stood in the hospital room with the family, minus the son. He had been told his father was critically ill, yet he hadn't come to see him. At the father's request, I called the son.

In Mark 7, we read about a man who was deaf. Not one sound had ever entered his ears. Not the voice of his parents, the rolling of thunder, or the singing of a bird at the break of dawn. And because hearing and speaking are directly related, this man's speech was also affected.

In verse 32, we read that people took him to Jesus and asked our merciful Lord to touch him. Jesus led the man away from the crowd for some privacy. Then He put His fingers into deaf ears and touched the impeded tongue. "'Ephphatha,' that is 'Be opened,'" Christ commanded (v. 34). Mercy and might were unleashed with those words! The man heard for the first time. He spoke clearly for the first time with words rolling off his tongue beautifully!

The voice of Christ is mighty. He speaks, and the deaf hear, the blind see, those who can't walk jump, the raging waves are stilled, the dead quiver with life, the hungry are fed, and so much more. The Lord's voice is never silenced, and His ears are always open, His words clear.

We can thank our gracious Lord for His voice of mercy! We are all like this man who was deaf. We have turned a deaf ear to the Lord and listened to the voices of this world. Lord, have mercy. We have spoken in worldly ways—untrue, unkind, uncaring, and ungodly words have rolled easily off our tongues. Lord, have mercy. We should be quick to listen, slow to speak (James 1:19). But we rearrange the order: quick to speak, slow to listen. Lord, have mercy. We turn a deaf ear to others, and words of anger pour forth from our lips. Gracious Lord, say to each one of us in mercy, "Ephphatha!" May we heed His words and not turn a deaf ear to Him.

"Sticks and stones may break my bones, but words shall never hurt me." This old rhyme is wrong. Words can cut to the depths of the heart. With our words, we can build one another up or tear one another down. We can tend to the wounds of others or inflict deeper wounds, instill hope or deliver crushing despair. Our words can be kind or cruel, true or false, godly or godless, combative or compassionate, loving or loveless, fitting or foul. We can deliver our words with stares, glares, frowns, or smiles. Our vocabulary in terms of words and nonverbal communication convey a great deal. We use thousands of words each day, but what are they and what is their intent? The Lord created us with a mind and a mouth. May they remain connected!

> **No human being can tame the tongue. It is a restless evil, full of deadly poison. With it we bless our Lord and Father, and with it we curse people who are made in the likeness of God. From the same mouth come blessing and cursing. My brothers, these things ought not to be so. (James 3:8–10)**

Yet it is so.

The tongue, so small, can inflict great damage. Words roll off your tongue and travel far and fast. The tongue does not consist of a single bone, yet it is so strong that it can mend or break someone's heart. It is so strong that it can deliver hope or instill dread, uplift or crush another's spirit. Consider these words of truth about the impact of our words:

> **Gracious words are like a honeycomb, sweetness to the soul and health to the body. (Proverbs 16:24)**

We should consider the tone that carries our words. Loud or soft? Kind or unkind? Loving or hateful? Uplifting or demeaning? With our words, we can lie, thereby communicating to another person that he or she is not important enough or trusted enough or loved enough to us. Every lie is satanic.

Rather than contemplate the number of words we speak, we should focus on their impact and purpose. Remember, every word we speak travels to a destination—someone's ear.

Unpleasant words are bitterness to the soul. Hurtful words hurt. We are to weigh our words before we speak, asking, "Why am I saying this? Is it helpful? Is it kind? Is it true?" Putting others down does not lift us up in any way. You certainly remember unpleasant words spoken to you and the wounds they delivered. Who said them to you? What faces come to mind? What words still inflict pain? Conversely, whose faces come into your mind when you think about those you have hurt with your words? Saying "No one" is a foul lie.

As we ponder our words, we should ask ourselves, "Why did I say that? What was the intention of my words?" To hurt? help? tear down? build up? We spoke, then thought. Many times, we didn't think at all. We gave a harsh answer to a soft question. Countless times, we have hurt others with wounds deep into their heart. We spoke in condescending tones to put another person in his or her place. Our lips moved in anger and arrogance. We have rudely put others down. We have given others the silent treatment, using the weapon of no words. Our words tell us loudly and clearly who we are: sinners. Our tongues have controlled us instead of controlling our tongues.

These three words should come from our lips: "Lord, forgive me." In light of our foul and unfitting words, there is a good word for us. He who is the Word in the flesh, Christ our Savior, speaks. The Holy Spirit gives us faith to open our ears so we can hear the Savior's voice. "Ephphatha!" His Word to you, sweeter than honey, is *forgiven.*

May the Lord of pardon grant us wisdom to think before we speak, to use our two ears more and our one tongue less; to offer the gifts of hope, forgiveness, care, and concern with our words; to keep heart, mind, and speech connected. May our words encourage rather than discourage, instill hope and not rob others of it, build one another up instead of tearing one another down, and convey Christ rather than crush reputations. May we give the gift of active listening to others.

There is such potential in our mouths for ill or good. There is a preponderance of words, but what are they? May that be the question we ask ourselves before we utter one single syllable. May we speak first to the Lord in prayer before uttering a single word to others, saying, "O Lord, open my lips, and my mouth will declare Your praise" (Psalm 51:15). Think, pray, speak.

TREASURE: Recall the beginning of this chapter and the family that had suffered division for so long. Everyone in the hospital room was aware that the father had asked me to reach out to the son. None of us knew how that phone call would go. We all know of estrangements that are never resolved, families that never reconcile.

"Hello?" the son answered.

"This is Pastor. I'm calling because your dad wants to speak to you. Would you please take his call?"

The son did, and words were exchanged—loving words. There were no verbal jabs or knockout punches. Instead, they each spoke powerful words of forgiveness and love. Within one hour, the son was in the hospital room. He embraced his dad, and they wept. "I'm so sorry." "Please forgive me." "I love you." The father died in his son's arms that afternoon.

Such words are rightly spoken in all families and all situations. For these are the words we speak to our Lord Jesus every day.

Take Heart

His Holy Word

Call to Me and I will answer you, and will tell you great and hidden things that you have not known. (Jeremiah 33:3)

Gracious words are like a honeycomb, sweetness to the soul and health to the body. (Proverbs 16:24)

Let no corrupting talk come out of your mouths, but only such as is good for building up, as fits the occasion, that it may give grace to those who hear. (Ephesians 4:29)

From the same mouth come blessing and cursing. My brothers, these things ought not to be so. (James 3:10)

A man who bears false witness against his neighbor is like a war club, or a sword, or a sharp arrow. (Proverbs 25:18)

Prayer

Gracious Lord, Your words are truth, love, and mercy. Open my ears to hear Your voice through Your Holy Word, and open my lips to declare Your praise. Forgive me for the foul and unfitting words I have spoken and for straining to listen to the foul words of this world while turning a deaf ear to You. Comfort me with Your word of pardon and mercy, Your voice of grace and truth, Your promise of forgiveness and eternal life. May I think, pray, and then speak. In Jesus' name. Amen.

CHAPTER 7

Satan's Defeat

MY TROUBLE: Satan's Deception
HIS TREASURE: Satan's Defeat

TROUBLE: It sounded like fun to go out with the guys, have a few beers, shoot a little pool, then go home to his wife and children. He thoughtfully phoned his wife, and she was fine with the idea. He was a hardworking husband who usually came straight home after work, so this was a rare treat. What could go wrong? Satan would set a trap with appealing bait. An attractive young woman sat just a table away.

He noticed her looking his way, and their eyes locked for a moment. Pleased with himself that he was still attractive, he engaged in a little small talk when she approached the pool table. It's no secret that small talk can lead to big problems. He thought about how lonely he felt in his marriage; his wife seemed to pay more attention to the kids than to him. He joined the woman at the bar for another beer. When the invitation to continue the conversation in her apartment was extended, he decided he could accept the offer and still be home in time to tuck the kids in at bedtime. The timing was perfect. He put the pool cue back in the rack and followed her.

After Jesus' Baptism in the Jordan River, He was driven by the Holy Spirit into the wilderness. He stood in the waters of the Jordan for you. Then He stood in the dry desert, tired and hungry, for you. For forty days, the Bread of Life ate nothing. Satan, fully aware of Jesus' physical hunger, tempted the Savior continually. The father of lies fired his darts, but he did not (could not) make them stick. "Hungry one, serve Yourself and turn these stones into bread." Never. "If You worship me, I will give You all the kingdoms of the world!" Never. "Test Your Father by jumping off the temple!" Never.

The devil left that scene, but until Good Friday, he never left our Lord alone.

The first Adam fell in Paradise. He listened to the one who hated him, not the One who loved him and his wife, Eve. Our first parents rejected the truth of the Creator in favor of the lies of the tempter. Their action brought sin, shame, guilt, death, and hell into the world. Paradise was shattered. God created an earthly garden, but now there are cemeteries.

The Second Adam, our Lord Jesus, who was true man, stood not in that garden but in the wilderness, and He was tired, hungry, and thirsty. But Our Lord's food is to do the will of God, who sent Him. Satan would have liked to have Christ avoid the cross, but Jesus came to earth and went to the cross. Jesus is Satan's full defeat, his ugly head crushed by the living feet of Christ. Jesus tells us,

I saw Satan fall like lightning from heaven. Behold, I have given you authority to tread on serpents and scorpions, and over all the power of the enemy, and nothing shall hurt you. Nevertheless, do not rejoice in this, that the spirits are subject to you, but rejoice that your names are written in heaven. (Luke 10:18–20)

Satan is defeated. However, the one who tempted our Lord most certainly tempts you time after time. For as much as the Lord loves you, Satan hates you. This is by necessity a blunt statement: the devil constantly prowls about looking for souls to devour—yours and mine and those of our loved ones. We chuckle at cartoons showing the devil with his horns and pitchfork, but this is no laughing matter. Satan has placed a bull's-eye on your back. He seeks to destroy your God-given faith in Christ. Yet you can be encouraged, because at your Baptism, you were marked with an indelible sign: the sign of the holy cross upon your forehead and your heart.

Remember: Jesus always speaks the truth, while Satan always lies. His foul lies are dressed as sweet and fragrant truth. Why do we tilt our ears away from the Lord and toward Satan? Why do we believe putrid untruth but question the pure truth of God's Word? Why are we so easily lured into the darkness and away from the light? "That will never happen to me. I am a strong Christian. I would never listen to the evil one."

Satan's lies can puff us up with deadly pride. He wants us to mount the high horse he sets in front of us. What a beautiful, muscular steed. Grab the reins, hop up, and ride on. The saddle is quite comfortable. From this seat, we can look down on others. "Giddy up. Let's go!" See the hapless drunk one in the gutter, the drug addict in the alley, the divorced loser, the poor neighbor. They are an embarrassment! Leave them all in a cloud of dust. Arm yourself with contempt and arrogance, and laugh as you point your finger at them. Losers! Ride on!

Satan whispers lies into our ears as we gallop along: "You are doing great. You are a winner. You are a good person. No, you are a great person. Remember, church is for losers. Why do you need to go? All they want is your money. The hymns and liturgy are boring. The pastor drones on and on. It's the same stuff every week." Satan lures us away from God's gifts of Word and Sacraments. Satan wants to sift you like wheat, to separate you from Christ, to destroy your faith.

In the face of these bold lies, hear this truth: you are no better than anyone else; no better than the drunk, the drug addict, the prostitute, the penniless, or anyone else. Little words make a big difference: "*All* have sinned and fall short of the glory God" (Romans 3:23, emphasis added).

I am a poor miserable sinner. So are you. So is the next person, and the next. You do not like what you are being told. Yet now you have ridden your high horse to death. His legs have buckled, and he is still. You rode on the back of a lie the whole time. You can dismount now. The ground is only inches away. There is no need to look down on others from this level of truth. Not one single human being ever belongs on a high horse.

The devil seeks to drive us from the light of Christ into the shadows and darkness of despair. He seeks to shove us into the damp, dark cave of hopelessness. There is no high horse in this dungeon. There are only foul lies that crush our spirit—lies that sound like this: "How could God ever love you, you worthless wretch." "Your sin is too great to ever be forgiven." "If God loved you, you wouldn't have these problems." We are trampled and pummeled by these vicious lies! The devil wants you face down in the darkness and dust of despair. He screams lies of failure and whispers lies of despair to us. We are no match for him.

Yet Satan is no match for Christ. None whatsoever! This is a most comforting truth. The One who was lifted high on the accursed tree crushed Satan. In His death on the cross, our Savior sunk down, down, down into unfathomable suffering in the dark depths of death for each of us. In the purest love, He who was rich became poor for our sake. He lifted not a single finger to protect Himself from shame but gave His back to the whip. His beard was given to those who plucked it out, His ears to those who cried, "Crucify Him, crucify Him!" He opened His hands for the nails. His mouth issued not a single complaint. He died zealously for you. He spilled His precious blood most willingly for you. Then He rose again bodily, mightily, victoriously. Satan is defeated; Jesus lives.

Christ is with you, and now Satan has no business bothering you. You are set free from the devil's lies and from his heavy and binding chains. Satan is trampled and crushed by the Savior. Jesus is the victor, not the victim. And you are not a hapless victim but a beloved a child of God. You are not in the dark shadows; rather, you stand in the unfading light of Christ and His love for you. Christ promises this, and His Word is truth. On your own, you have no chance against the devil—but you are never alone. Christ is with you always, to the end of the age and still after that!

One little name fells Satan every time: *Jesus.* This name is above every name! Use it! Pray, "Father, lead me not into temptation. In Jesus' name." Remember your Baptism and take heart. In your Baptism, you received the armor of God—the breastplate of righteousness, the helmet of salvation, the shield of faith, and the sword of the spirit, which is the Word of God (Ephesians 6:10–20)—and God's protection from the devil's evil plots, plans, and ploys. Read God's Holy Word and receive the Lord's Supper, which fit you from head to toe with offensive and defensive weapons to "extinguish all the flaming darts of the evil one" (Ephesians 6:16). You have Jesus. Better said, Jesus has you—in His full armor.

TREASURE: Recall the man we met at the beginning of this chapter. He left the bar. Alone. Thanks be to God, he went straight home to his wife and children. He saw the darkness, darts, and danger that had been concealed with a seductive smile and invitation as nothing other than Satan's foul lies all dressed up as "a good time."

There is no right way to do a wrong thing. And it is never wrong to do the right thing. The darts of temptation bounce off the shield of faith and fall uselessly to the ground. Another foul plot by the devil is foiled. This husband went home and fell into the arms of his wife.

Take Heart

Satan's Defeat

Be sober-minded; be watchful. Your adversary the devil prowls around like a roaring lion, seeking someone to devour. (1 Peter 5:8)

Submit yourselves therefore to God. Resist the devil, and he will flee from you. (James 4:7)

No temptation has overtaken you that is not common to man. God is faithful, and He will not let you be tempted beyond your ability, but with the temptation He will also provide the way of escape, that you may be able to endure it. (1 Corinthians 10:13)

Lead us not into temptation, but deliver us from evil. (Matthew 6:13)

But the Lord is faithful. He will establish you and guard you against the evil one. (2 Thessalonians 3:3)

Prayer

Risen Savior, Jesus Christ, with Your bloody death and bodily resurrection, Satan's head is crushed triumphantly and thoroughly. You are the victor and share the spoils with me. My own sinful heart has led me astray. I have given in to temptation countless times and have made excuses for my sin. This You know full well, my Lord. Forgive me. Refresh me with Your profuse love and lead me in Your paths. Keep the evil one far from me and carry me safely in Your loving arms, for You are my shield and strength. In Your holy name. Amen.

CHAPTER 8

Marriage

MY TROUBLE: My Marriage
HIS TREASURE: My Marriage

TROUBLE: When I first met them, the young couple had been excited, and rightfully so. Over the next few months, they completed premarriage counseling and planned their wedding service. Then the day of their marriage arrived, and the Lord's house was filled with their family and friends. They spoke their vows joyfully. This doesn't sound like trouble at all. But hold on! Only a few years later, I got a phone call from the bride. "I want a ____________," she cried.

All was perfect at creation. The Lord, who called all things into existence from nothing, declared it to be "very good." But hold on! One thing was not good, as the Lord Himself stated: "It is not good that the man should be alone" (Genesis 2:18). So Adam would not be alone. The Creator gave Adam a most precious gift—Eve, taken from his very side. It was the first marriage, but not the last! So we speak of Adam and Eve, Abraham and Sarah, Isaac and Rebecca, Joseph and Mary, you and ____________. Not by chance or mere circumstance, the Lord brings man and woman together and blesses the union.

If you are married, what words would you use to characterize your life with your spouse? Do you remember how your wedding day was full of hope and promise? You spoke your vows clearly and joyfully. The wedding rings sparkled magnificently. The bride was beautiful, and the groom handsome. The reception was wonderful, the cake was moist and tasty. The toasts were so well spoken, and the glasses were lifted high. Your future was bright. How you beamed as you were introduced as Mr. and Mrs. There was laughter and tears of joy and prayers of thanksgiving.

That was then; this is now. Whether your marriage was years or months ago, perhaps the shadows are lengthening as if the sun is setting on your marriage. Maybe you and your spouse have drifted apart. A cold front has settled in. There is no laughter and little communication. There may even be many arguments. There are still tears, but now they are of pain and hurt and frustration. You find that you and your spouse are blaming and bullying each other. You have grown disillusioned, thinking things will never be better. What happened? Where did the romance go? Where did the love go? The good days of your marriage are in the distant past, and now divorce creeps into your thoughts. How have you and your spouse become enemies? You search on your phone for the number of that lawyer your friend told you about. As you do, an old friend's face flashes in your mind. Where is that person these days? Your marriage, once fresh and vibrant, is now a shriveled leaf.

What troubles me about my marriage is that __________ ____.

Here are some things to think about instead of abandoning your marriage.

You and your spouse are both sinners. There is no perfect marriage, for there is no perfect person. Those movie romances are not reality but are made for entertainment purposes. The pop songs have catchy lyrics but are made to raise expectations to an unreachable level. One key to a lasting marriage is spouses who forgive each other. They readily say, "I am sorry. Will you forgive me?" Consider how you have contributed to the problems in your marriage and how you can now contribute to the solution.

Love keeps no record of wrongs. We lovelessly do. We keep a precise, detailed record of every word and action that upset us. Time, date, and place are noted. Again and again and again. A husband reminds his wife of something she said years ago that he disliked. The wife in turn reminds him of something he did that she didn't like. The battle of words continues with no resolution. Day after day, year after year. The accusations fly: "You could have; you should have." "You did; you didn't." You give your spouse a piece of your mind and none of your heart. Put down your pen and stop keeping track. Confess your wrongdoing and own it. Forgive your spouse and mean it. Stop yelling. "Be kind to one another, tenderhearted, forgiving one another, as Christ forgave you" (Ephesians 4:32). "Please forgive me" and "I do forgive you" are powerful words of love. Say them! A day without love and forgiveness is a wasted day. Remember that lost time is never found. What have your words conveyed to your spouse? What do your words say about you?

We equate love with feelings, which places love on a shaky foundation. Feelings change, vacillate, come and go, ebb and flow. We don't always feel like going to work. We don't always feel excited at a ballgame. We don't always feel overjoyed at home, like going to church, like going to the gym. Love based on feelings is tenuous at best.

The rich and productive soil in which the taproot of a marriage grows is not emotion. It is commitment. It is a husband or wife saying, "I am not giving up. I will work through this with you. We will come out stronger on the other side." But far too many people give up too soon. Instead of growing and learning in their marriage, they simply switch spouses and are surprised if the circumstances transpire again. Today is difficult. Tomorrow can be better. Those who throw the "I quit" card on the table and walk away will never know what the future may have held.

Marriage takes work. A troubled marriage is a summons to change things. First, it is a call to remember that marriage is a blessing from the Lord and is blessed by the Lord. Examine your own heart and acknowledge how you may have hurt your spouse or contributed to the difficulties of your marriage. Ask for forgiveness. Speak forgiveness. Talk, but listen more. Resolve to address problems in love and do not create problems in anger. Stop criticizing and start encouraging. Anger causes multiple problems and does not solve a single one. Where does sinful anger lead you? To court, or to the arms of your spouse?

Second, spend quality time together, not in front of a screen but tuned into each other in a quiet setting. Look at each other! Date again and recapture the joy of your early life together. Win your spouse's heart again with kindness and respect. Listen to your spouse. Then listen some more. Stop being right, and start being kind. Continue to build intimacy through seemingly small things, such as a hug, a word of kindness, a shared memory. Say "thank you." Stop with the put-downs and pick up affirmative words. Kindness and thankfulness cause the spirit of your spouse to soar and improves the atmosphere of your home. Kindness begets kindness; forgiveness begets forgiveness. Take hold of that hand! To do these little things consistently is better than to do big things such as flowers once a year on Valentines' Day or a preprinted greeting card on your anniversary.

Guard your home as a haven from the callous world, a secure safe harbor of care in a careless world. Work to make your home a place you and your loved ones want to return to. Many people have houses. Not all have a home. Enjoy each other's company. Communicate. Be patient. Forgive. Do things that draw you closer together. Home sweet home! Seek that punctuation mark. Your home should be a place of warmth in a cold society, a soft place to land in a hardened world. Do your part to make your home a place of encouragement and enjoyment, with the emotional thermostat turned to warm. A Christian home is a place of love and forgiveness in a world that extols hatred and vengeance. We are reminded of the importance of a caring atmosphere in our homes with these words: "Better is a dinner of herbs where love is than a fattened ox and hatred with it" (Proverbs 15:17).

Marriage isn't easy, but it is a blessing. In the marriage ceremony, the Lord sanctifies the union—He declares the marriage to be holy. Divorce painfully rips apart that union. When one or both people in a marriage quit the union, both husband

and wife are hurt deeply to the very core. Children, regardless of age, bear a heavy weight when their parents get divorced. A troubled relationship is an unmistakable summons to grow and change. Grow. Do not give up. A wilting marriage is refreshed by turning to Christ. A tree that is not watered dies. The cord of three strands, a familiar metaphor in marriage ceremonies, is you, your spouse, and Christ, with His refreshing and replenishing love. Ecclesiastes 4:12 tells us that such a cord is not easily broken. Separating the strands—removing Christ—weakens marriage. Two strands are not so durable and may not hold against the stressors of the world.

The counsel of the world concerning a troubled marriage is to quit, to go it alone, to put oneself first, and to not worry about how the separation may affect the rest of the family. The world says to love yourself, to just be happy. To be sure, some marriages are not healthy and should not be preserved. Infidelity, abuse, abandonment, or addiction can be fatal to a marriage if the person guilty of these sins is unrepentant and unwilling to make amends.

Generally speaking, the world would have us believe that marriage is more about the trappings of weddings than about the blessings of the union. Some people have even believed the worldly lie that marriage isn't necessary and is old-fashioned—that consenting adults can simply live together without the hassle of getting married. None of this is God's way, however. None of it.

A successful marriage is not one that is free of trouble. Rather, it is one where husband and wife humble themselves before each other, acknowledge their mistakes, and seek forgiveness. Premarriage counseling is a blessing to couples who are just starting out. The importance of godly decision-making cannot be discounted, and a pastor's guidance can be the difference for a marriage that begins with realistic expectations and with Christ at the center. Pastoral counsel can help couples learn to resolve conflicts, grow together in faith, and navigate challenges at any time through their life together.

Among us there is no perfect husband, wife, marriage, or family. We have all failed miserably. Our hope lies with the perfect Bridegroom, Christ, who loves us. Indeed, He loved His Bride to death. His Bride, though, was ugly with sin from head to toe, covered with foul blemishes, dressed in putrid rags, and unlovable. She was unfaithful (see Hosea 2), yet faithful Christ loved her. The beauty of His love replaces the ugliness of her sin. He has adorned His Bride in the stainless, spotless garments of salvation. He says, "I will betroth you to Me forever" (Hosea 2:19). He does not abandon you or break His promises to you. He who turned water into the finest wine at the wedding in Cana will provide His finest for you and your marriage. In Him, there is unlimited forgiveness, mercy, grace, and love for you, your spouse, your marriage, your family. "Oh, taste and see that the Lord is good!" (Psalm 34:8).

Before turning to the divorce lawyer, return to the Lord. He mends and strengthens the ties that bind. You can take heart, for Christ will provide for you—without fail. Ask the couple at Cana and their wedding guests. Then lift a glass to better days.

Now, what gives me hope for my marriage is ___________
____.

TREASURE: Divorce. Think back to beginning of this chapter and the couple that came in for marriage counseling. They valued their marriage enough to work on things. In our counseling sessions, we reviewed the Bible basics of grace, mercy, confession, forgiveness, repentance, and love. And they were honest with themselves and each other. She confessed that marriage wasn't what she thought it would be. She thought they would frequently go out to dinner, travel. She thought he would bring her gifts and flowers and would always be in a good mood. He wasn't; nor was she.

We went back to the basics: God sanctified and blessed their union. They spoke vows to each other and to God.

We talked about the God-given vocations of husband and wife and the responsibility to forgive, commit, love, and work through things. We discussed that the Lord blessed their union and that they had vowed to be together until death parted them. Then they talked *to* each other and not *at* each other. They each owned how they contributed to the problems in their marriage. Through these discussions, they began to rebuild their marriage with the mortar of God's love. They turned to Christ and His love, to forgiveness, commitment, and contentment. These are the bedrock of marriage. Are they still married? Indeed. They have celebrated their twenty-fifth anniversary. Praise be to God!

Every marriage has ups and downs. Your marriage vows don't change, but you do. Marriage is no fairy tale with a perfect prince and princess. There is no carriage waiting to ride off to happily ever after.

But there *is* Christ and His love. The Lord keeps His vows to you, and as you come to His house to hear the Gospel proclaimed and receive His Holy Meal, the blessings overflow into your marriage. Work on your marriage by turning to the Lord and asking Him to help you. Kindness begets kindness! Tell yourself and your spouse, "With the help of God, we will recommit and work to save this marriage."

"Lord, in Your mercy, hear our prayer."

Take Heart

My Marriage

I will betroth you to Me forever. I will betroth you to Me in righteousness and in justice, in steadfast love and in mercy. (Hosea 2:19)

For your Maker is your husband, the LORD of hosts is His name; and the Holy One of Israel is your Redeemer, the God of the whole earth He is called. (Isaiah 54:5)

Then the LORD God said, "It is not good that the man should be alone; I will make him a helper fit for him." (Genesis 2:18)

But the fruit of the Spirit is love, joy, peace, patience, kindness, goodness, faithfulness, gentleness, self-control; against such things there is no law. (Galatians 5:22–23)

Therefore a man shall leave his father and mother and hold fast to his wife, and the two shall become one flesh. (Ephesians 5:31)

Prayer

Lord Jesus, You love Your Bride, having washed her in Your holy blood. You are the perfect Bridegroom—ever faithful, ever loving, ever providing. You clothe her in Your own robes of righteousness. Thank You for the gift of marriage—one man, one woman for one lifetime. Deepen the bonds between husband and wife. Bless our homes with Your presence and grant abiding love between husband and wife so that our homes may be bastions of love in a loveless world. In Your holy name. Amen.

CHAPTER 9

Daily Bread

MY TROUBLE: Greed

HIS TREASURE: Daily Bread

TROUBLE: In a lively discussion, one of the members of the congregation asked if I had seen the billboard along the highway west of town. I hadn't. "Well, it makes a good case for playing the lottery," he stated. He added, "My life would really change if I won. I would give some of the millions to the congregation, of course."

He was talking about the odds of winning the lottery and about his generous nature. "There are no odds with the Lord," I responded. "He always provides for you, for me, and for this congregation. No odds, no losers, no ticket required. The lottery—no. The Lord's providence—yes."

"Well, drive by and look at the billboard," he quipped. "You might change your mind." This gentleman and I had numerous discussions about the lottery over the years. Americans spend tens of billions of dollars on lottery tickets annually, with the hope of making their daily lives better. At the same time, we petition our heavenly Father to "give us this day our daily bread."

Daily is a great word that points to a great, giving God and eliminates the insatiable need to stockpile treasures for the future. The Lord gives *daily* without exception or restraint. *Bread* is also great word that includes all we need to support this body and life: food, shelter, clothing, safety, money, and so on. Moment by moment, the Bread of Life cares for you, providing lavishly for your body and soul. The petition "give us this day" is a stark contrast to the greedy "I want more" because it acknowledges that the Lord provides what we need in this moment. Daily bread is ours from His loving, generous hand.

We are the greedy ones, always wanting more, always worried about the future, always reluctant to share. But what do we lack with Christ? Nothing. What do we have with Christ? Everything, now and for all eternity! All we are and have is a gift from our gracious, great, and giving God.

Our Creator gave us a perfect world where there was no sickness, hunger, hurt, or fear. But the father of lies asked, "Did God actually say . . . ?" (Genesis 3:1) and introduced the notion that God was holding out on us. Sin brought with it toil, hardship, illness, war, and death. Now, untold multitudes live in poverty and succumb to bodily need. There are no doubt people in our community, neighborhood, congregation, and, perhaps, immediate family who go without basics like food, shelter, and medical care. At the same time, the Lord has blessed untold others with more than enough. May our compassionate Lord move us all to respond with love and mercy in service to others according to His will.

But the devil wants us to want more, and he knows that

want can displace need. This happens when we mistakenly and sinfully believe that things like winning the lottery will make all the difference in our lives, especially that wealth will make us happy. When we are never satisfied with what God has given us, when we think that if we have just a little bit more or a little more after that, then we will have enough, that's when we have made "more" our idol. Our sinful nature tells us that enough is never enough. We should remember that greed is the love God hates.

King Belshazzar of Babylon knew about greed. In Daniel 5, we read that the king had everything—jewels, riches, beautiful robes, food, drink, a castle with safe, thick walls. To show off his wealth, Belshazzar held a great feast for a thousand of his lords and his wives and concubines. He was also thumbing his nose at the enemy that was camped just outside the city wall. Proud and defiant, the king took a sip of wine in front of the crowd. Then he ordered his guests to drink wine from silver and gold vessels. These sacred vessels, stolen from the temple in Jerusalem, were now used at a pagan feast in an act of deliberate insult to the God of Israel. At Belshazzar's command, all those present "drank wine and praised the gods of gold and silver, bronze, iron, wood, and stone" (Daniel 5:4). What a king! What a party!

Belshazzar must have smiled broadly as he watched the vessels lifted high and then lowered to the lips of servants, wives, and concubines. He had his things, his people, his power. Yet of what avail are these when one breathes his final breath?

Suddenly, the party was interrupted. The fingers of a man's hand appeared and wrote on the plaster wall of the palace: *Mene, Mene, Tekel, Parsin.* Belshazzar's face grew pale, his knees knocked, and his legs gave out in utter fear. "Bring in the astrologers!" he cried out. "If anyone can figure out the handwriting on the wall, I will reward him with fine clothes and gold and give him a high-ranking position in my kingdom!"

Not one of the Babylonian astrologers or soothsayers could understand the words. Now what? Who could interpret the words? The queen had an idea: "There is a man in your kingdom in whom is the spirit of the holy gods" (Daniel 5:11). His name: Daniel.

An Israelite exile, Daniel was known for his wisdom and ability to interpret dreams. He had served in Nebuchadnezzar's court for many years, and now he was an old man. In short order, the king and Daniel were face to face, and Daniel knew that the handwriting was on the wall for Belshazzar literally. He said, "You have lifted up yourself against the Lord of heaven. And the vessels of His house have been brought in before you, and you and your lords, your wives, and your concubines have drunk wine from them. And you have praised the gods of silver and gold, of bronze, iron, wood, and stone, which do not see or hear or know, but the God in whose hand is your breath, and whose are all your ways, you have not honored" (Daniel 5:23).

Daniel went on to tell Belshazzar that the words on the wall were from God. He gave the meaning of each word:

> **Mene, God has numbered the days of your kingdom and brought it to an end;**
>
> **Tekel, you have been weighed in the balances and found wanting;**

Peres, your kingdom is divided and given to the Medes and Persians. (Daniel 5:26)

What now? Belshazzar was murdered that very evening. All his riches and his gods could not protect him. This account prompts us to ask what is more important in life—what we have or who we are? What is more important in death—what we have or what we believe? Our Lord reminds us, "Take care, and be on your guard against all covetousness, for one's life does not consist in the abundance of his possessions" (Luke 12:15). A hearse doesn't have a hitch to pull a U-Haul.

We chase after things our whole lives. A child wants a trike, then a bicycle. As the years pass, a young adult wants a car, then a better car, then a house, then a bigger house. On and on this goes. After school, a job, a promotion. Perhaps marriage and children. Perhaps a vacation, and then a bigger vacation. Retirement, old age, and death.

And then? When we draw our last breath, the possessions we have don't matter. Our goods and money are useless; they avail us nothing. We think about the now and rarely about the "and then." Right now, ponder your future, not the present. The poorest man has only money. On our deathbed, it is not the what that matters—it's the who: Christ Jesus.

Only Christ Jesus matters now. He humbly took on our flesh, was born, and was laid in a manger. And then? He stood in the Jordan to be baptized. And then He willingly was crucified for us. And then He died. But then He rose again, ascended into heaven, and sits at God the Father's right hand. And then? He will come again. His grace and mercy will carry us to the place He has prepared for us.

With the gift of faith in Christ, we have the undeserved and unearned gifts of forgiveness, redemption, peace, and eternal life. These precious gifts cannot be bought or sold, merited, or warranted. As Christians, then, our focus is not on gold but on God's grace; not on lucre but on love; not on money but on mercy. Take heart! These are the true treasures and purest of gifts that avail us everything right now, for all our tomorrows, and then, for all eternity. How rich we are! We lack nothing, for in Christ, we have everything. The Bread of Life sets a full table before us daily.

TREASURE: A newscast showed a man holding a check for twenty million dollars he had won playing the lottery. Is this a good case for buying a lottery ticket? I don't think so. Although I don't know what he did with all that money, and I don't know if his life was improved exponentially, I think the lottery is a billboard for greed. Lottery revenue fills state coffers, funds important programs, and generates conversation. But the lottery also inspires idolatry, for it makes money a god.

"What did you think?" the man who advocated the lottery asked me. "Are you convinced now?"

"Maybe they should put up billboards for all the people who have lost money buying lottery tickets," I said. "The losing tickets would stretch across the whole state and back again and again and again. It is the Lord who fills our hands, my friend. Not the lottery and empty pockets."

Praise be to God that he understood.

Take Heart

Daily Bread

My God will supply every need of yours according to His riches in glory in Christ Jesus. (Philippians 4:19)

If you then, who are evil, know how to give good gifts to your children, how much more will your Father who is in heaven give good things to those who ask Him! (Matthew 7:11)

The eyes of all look to You, and You give them their food in due season. You open Your hand; You satisfy the desire of every living thing. (Psalm 145:15–16)

I am the LORD your God, who brought you up out of the land of Egypt. Open your mouth wide, and I will fill it. (Psalm 81:10)

He who did not spare His own Son but gave Him up for us all, how will He not also with Him graciously give us all things? (Romans 8:32)

Prayer

Heavenly Father, You graciously open Your hand and give me daily bread, providing for all of my needs of body and soul. Your goodness knows no limits, nor does Your love, for You gave Your Son, Jesus Christ, to suffer, bleed, and die for my sake. Forgive my sinful greed. My name is carved on Your living hand, right next to the nail mark. I deserve nothing, but You give me everything. Daily bread is mine from He who is the Bread of Life, my living Savior, Jesus Christ. Lavish is His love and provision for me. In His holy name I pray. Amen.

CHAPTER 10

My Cup Runneth Over

MY TROUBLE: Negativity

HIS TREASURE: Provision

TROUBLE: Have you ever met someone who casts everything in the shadows of negativity? Misery loves company, as they say, and we can all fall into the kind of thinking that sees problems as immense and the possibility of overcoming them as minute. It is as if we are blind to God's blessings and unaware of His provision for His people. This reminds me of a council member at a neighboring congregation. Their pastor had recently accepted a call to another congregation, and the church council was discussing the impending vacancy. Negativity dripped from one man's mouth.

"No one will ever come here," he said. "We are too small, and we can't pay a pastor enough. That district salary scale is ridiculously high." He cast the previous pastor negatively with comments such as "His sermons were too long" and "His pants had stains on them" and "His children were way too loud."

Every word the man spoke was negative, from the weather (too cold) to the economy (too slow) to the car I drove (too old).

Every meeting and every conversation with him was negative. One day, when just the two of us were in the room, I decided to chime in. "You're right. The salary scale is too high. The road driving here has way too many potholes, and that makes my old car really rattle. By the way, have you heard of the Menske people who are relocating here in a few months? They come from somewhere in the South Pacific. I heard they don't work too hard and expect handouts like food and housing."

"I know," the man said. "I have heard about them, and I am not happy they will be coming here."

Ask yourself how you would feel about the Menske people moving next to you.

The proverbial question "Is the glass half full or half empty?" is best answered with *yes*. The answer is simply a matter of perspective. A positive perspective is that the glass is half full. A negative perspective is that the glass is half empty. A despairing person might say, "I don't even have a glass." Negative words come from our own mouths: "There is no hope for me." Negativity comes from the mouths of others into our own ears: "There is no hope for you." What is your perspective? Are you an optimist or a pessimist? Do you feel hopeful or hopeless? How do you see the glass: half full or half empty? Ask yourself why you answer the way you do. Does your answer change with circumstances?

It is sad that some people make the worst of every situation. At times, we can all have a sour attitude. Generally speaking, negativity rules our world day and night. The sky is clear blue, but the forecast is for rain. The hot meal is too hot; the spicy chicken is too spicy. The rich color of the rose is offset by thorns. We stand in front of the open door of our full refrigerator and mutter, "There is nothing to eat." Naysayers responding to your new idea tell you, "It will never work." Our toast always falls jelly-side down. Splat.

To teach a lesson in negativity, I hold up a sheet of white paper with a black ink dot in the middle. "What do you see?" I ask. The most common answer people give is that they see a black dot. Although the rest of the piece of paper is white, they focus on the tiny black dot. We all tend to look at the negative in our lives, while the great positives go unnoticed. One tiny black dot becomes the singular focus.

This focus on the negative was introduced with the serpent's suggestion to Eve that there was something better. She turned toward the black dot of doubt and away from the vast perfection of God's creation. The result was dissatisfaction with God's provision. From that moment on, we have focused only on what's broken and not on what is good. We are critical of ourselves and of others. And the devil relentlessly points out what's wrong in the world. He directs our attention toward imperfections and tries to convince us we are worthless, unlovable, and irredeemable. There is no hope, he says. The world is doomed, he cackles. What is there to feel good about?

We can feel good about the fact that our heavenly Father promises—and delivers—an endless amount of good to His people. Think of this passage: "Rejoice in the Lord always; again I will say, rejoice" (Philippians 4:4). Notice there is no mention of Paul's circumstances. He does not say, "Rejoice because things are going well," but simply, "Rejoice." He says it twice for emphasis.

Do you know the situation Paul was in when he wrote those words? Was he in a penthouse or a prison? Was he looking at a scenic vista or dungeon walls? Philippians 1:13 mentions guards and chains, so we know that Paul was in prison when he wrote this letter. First-century Roman prisons were likely filthy, dank, crowded, and poorly ventilated. Paul was in dire circumstances. But he did not focus on a black dot. Rather, he focused on the bright light of Christ and His grace. He did not rejoice in his circumstances, which can change, but in the changeless Christ and His love in all circumstances. Thus, one can rejoice in the cemetery, the hospital, the unemployment line, the prison, the disaster aftermath—this is an astounding truth! The ointment for our wounds is Christ.

Paul's words to the Philippians did not sugarcoat his sour situation. For him, the glass was full, even in prison. Could his hope be snuffed out by negativity? Could a cellmate say, "What are you talking about, you fool? This cell is dark, damp, and dingy. Don't you shiver at night? The smell is atrocious. The food, that is, the few crumbs we get, is not fit for animals. Speaking of animals, rats crawl through these cramped quarters all night long. My sores are festering with infection. The guards are mean and abusive. I miss my wife and children. We could be killed at any moment. And you, a nutjob, say 'rejoice?' What glass do you see, fella? There isn't one!"

Yes, Paul's glass—his attitude toward his life—was full to the point of running over. Habakkuk the prophet would agree. His circumstances were dire: "Though the fig tree should not blossom, nor fruit be on the vines, the produce of the olive fail and the fields yield no food, the flock be cut off from the fold and there be no herd in the stalls, yet I will rejoice in the LORD; I will take joy in the God of my salvation" (Habakkuk 3:17–18).

Paul was confined in prison and breathed stale air. Habakkuk could freely roam the countryside and breathe the fresh air. Yet there were black dots in his landscape:

No blossoms on the fig tree.

No fruit on the vines.

No olives.

No crop in the field.

A cut-off flock.

Empty stalls.

Does he have hope? Habakkuk professed, "Yet I will rejoice in the LORD." Despite the horrible situation—no blossoms, no fruit, no olives, no crop, no herd—he did not despair. Where was the negativity, the self-pity, the foot stomping? Did he say, "I deserve better than this!" Or "God, how could You do this to me?" Read the passage again. One word comes into clear focus: *rejoice*. He did not say to wait for some distant day when fruit and olives appeared again, when livestock was in the stalls, when starvation was no longer imminent. No! This prophet of God said to rejoice in the Lord and His unchanging love. Right here, right now—in these present circumstances. Habakkuk rejoiced; you can too.

We rejoice in Christ and His changeless love for us. Our circumstances change, but the love of Christ is changeless. Jesus drank the cup of woe to the very last drop. Take heart, for He extends to you the full cup of salvation. Drink deeply. Difficulties are above us, below us, in front of us, and behind us. Every single minute of every single day presents challenges. Relentless trials and troubles hound us. In this life, there is always something to complain about. But Christ quenches you with His living water and carries you in His arms. You can always rejoice in the Lord of your salvation, whether the sky is blue or gray, whether the barn is full or empty. Ask Paul. Ask Habakkuk. Ask God. Pray for the Holy Spirit to turn your heart away from the doom and gloom of earthly life and toward the hope that is yours in Jesus.

Be assured that even those who do not see past the black dot are still God's beloved children, still forgiven by our Savior's work on the cross. Our heavenly Father loves us whether we are cranky or happy, whether we have a negative attitude or a positive one. Therefore, let us strive to keep uppermost in our mind Paul's words to the church in Philippi:

> **The peace of God, which surpasses all understanding, will guard your hearts and your minds in Christ Jesus.**
>
> **Finally, brothers, whatever is true, whatever is honorable, whatever is just, whatever is pure, whatever is lovely, whatever is commendable, if there is any excellence, if there is anything worthy of praise, think about these things. (Philippians 4:7–8)**

TREASURE: "About the Menske people . . ." Think back to the chronically negative man at the beginning of this chapter. I had to confess to him that I had made up the story about the Menske people moving to our community. I didn't do this to be mean but to show him how his thinking had darkened his attitude toward his world and infected those he spoke with. "There are no such people," I said. "Yet you were immediately negative about them. In fact, every situation and person is cast in a critical light every time you speak. I hear you talking about what is wrong, but you never talk about what is right. There is a better way."

I would see this man many times through the years. He changed. Thanks be to God! When he spoke, it was positive. He became a blessing! One night after another congregational meeting, he said to me with a wry smile, "Be safe driving home. Not to be negative, but it is cold." He was right—it was 22 degrees below zero!

Take Heart

Provision

You prepare a table before me in the presence of my enemies; You anoint my head with oil; my cup overflows. (Psalm 23:5)

Finally, brothers, whatever is true, whatever is honorable, whatever is just, whatever is pure, whatever is lovely, whatever is commendable, if there is any excellence, if there is anything worthy of praise, think about these things. (Philippians 4:8)

Count it all joy, my brothers, when you meet trials of various kinds. (James 1:2)

I will praise the name of God with a song; I will magnify Him with thanksgiving. (Psalm 69:30)

Like a lame man's legs, which hang useless, is a proverb in the mouth of fools. (Proverbs 26:7)

Prayer

Gracious and giving Savior, I have every reason to rejoice in every circumstance, for You are always good to me. You will never leave me nor forsake me. Your hand is never closed in indifference to me, nor is Your face ever turned away from me. I lack nothing with You and Your love. Yet I have sinfully complained. I have been ungrateful. I have been negative. My words expose my ingratitude and negativity. Forgive me. With Habakkuk, may I say, "I will rejoice in the LORD; I will take joy in the God of my salvation" (Habakkuk 3:18), even if there is no crop in the field and no herd in the stalls. Your love is my greatest gift. My cup forever runneth over. In Jesus' name. Amen.

CHAPTER 11

Humility

MY TROUBLE: Their Hypocrisy (No, Mine)

HIS TREASURE: Humility

TROUBLE: The time for Thursday morning Bible class had arrived. We were studying the book of Isaiah. The regular attendees arrived and took their seats. I was shuffling through my notes and reviewing a few items at the podium. I glanced at my watch: 8:54 a.m. Six minutes to go. Then *he* walked in. His photograph had been on the front page of our local newspaper, accompanied by an article about his crime of being a thief in the business world. He had been found guilty, served his time in state prison, paid his price to society, and been released from prison. Through it all, he had lost his family, his business, and his reputation. Now he was coming to Bible class!

Well and good. But a regular attendee in the class asked to speak with me privately at the front of the room. She spoke in soft tones at first but grew increasingly louder: "What is *he* doing here? He has no business walking through the door of this church! He shouldn't even be a member here! He should have been dropped from the rolls. He embarrassed all of us. He needs to leave now! Pastor, tell him to go!"

The humility of Christ is a wonder to behold. He, the Creator of all, was carried within the confines of a womb. He, the light of the world, was born on a dark Judean night and laid in a manger. There was no palace, no armed guards, no feather bed, no room for Him in the inn. There was—and is—above all, love for you in the flesh. Jesus, true God from all eternity, clothed Himself in our blood and bone. The eternal One entered time for our sake, not His. Jesus was born for our sake, and He was born to die. He came to rescue and redeem. Our Lord's birth certificate in Bethlehem yielded to His death certificate in Jerusalem, signed with His own precious blood.

Our Lord had nowhere to lay His sacred head. He had no comeliness that one should seek Him. He is the King who rode into Jerusalem not with pomp and circumstance, not with sword and spear, not with white steeds and armed soldiers. He was armed only with love, bearing His cross. He rode in to die. He came for you.

Jesus is the King whose place—not *palace*—was a cross on Golgotha, a hill of torment and death for sentenced criminals. This was the locale of the guilty and the condemned. The sinless One went here to take our sin. The King was crowned with thorns. He gave His life breath and precious blood for you, for He "emptied Himself, by taking the form of a servant, being born in the likeness of men. And being found in human form, He humbled Himself by becoming obedient to the point of death, even death on a cross" (Philippians 2:7–8). Our Lord had nowhere to lay His sacred head other than on this beam of wood. He did so most lovingly.

The opposite of humility is pride. Consider this scenario: A man walked into the room with the utmost confidence and approached the podium with his head held high. The room fell silent as those present straightened in their seats to listen better. The man, a doctor of theology, prepared to begin. First, he checked the printed program to make sure "ThD" was after his name. After all, that was of utmost importance. He would now proceed to dispense his profound wisdom to the simpletons gathered in front of him. The applause for him was deafening. He scanned the audience with approval as he straightened his clerical collar.

Another man sat in a dark alley alone. He had crawled there from the street corner only minutes before. He had lost all confidence long ago. He raised the whiskey bottle to his lips with quivering hands. There was one last good chug left. The only sound around him was that of rats digging through piles of trash. His thoughts were scattered, but the regret of a failed marriage and a ruined career predominated. He straightened the dirty, ragged scarf around his neck, his head held low.

The doctor of theology had been chauffeured to the auditorium from the airport, his route passing by the alley where the man in the scarf sat. Glancing out the car window, the eyes of the doctor caught a glimpse of the pitiful situation. He, however, was pitiless. *Worthless drunk,* he thought, again adjusting his clerical collar.

The alley was quiet, other than the scurrying of rats, and it was lonely. There was no applause or crowd of people here. The alley dweller found a half-eaten hamburger in the pile of trash.

The long applause slowly died down, and the doctor cleared

his throat and began his tutelage. He spoke of *simplicitas Dei*, *genus apotelesmaticum*, *quiniscient*, and *operate attributes*, *cultus ara divinus*, and *voluntas prima*, *sive antecedens*, *et volutas*, *secunda*, *sive consequences*, and more. The people were impressed with his deep insights as Latin rolled off the lips of the learned scholar. The audience sat in awe of his wisdom, even as they were unsure of what he was really talking about.

A cold wind blew down the alley. The hamburger still had ketchup and part of pickle on it. A treasure found in the trash! Two soiled hands came together, folded in prayer. "Lord Jesus, have mercy. Thank You for Your bountiful goodness to me, a poor, miserable sinner. Bless this food that You have provided. Amen." Two bites and the meal was over.

After his lecture, the doctor was driven back to his hotel by a student who had been in attendance. "You are a very learned man," the student said. "I so enjoyed your wisdom. Your knowledge of Latin is amazing."

"How much further to the hotel?" the doctor impatiently replied. His stomach had started to growl. Soon he was sitting at a fancy table in the hotel restaurant with a steak set before him. He dove right in. But after one bite, he shouted for the waiter to come over. "I ordered a well-done steak. This is medium! Where is the manager of this rat trap?" The clamor caused other patrons to look at the man in the white clerical collar with a red face and a loud angry voice. The doctor slammed his fork on the table, stormed out, and went to his room.

He decided to take a walk before he polished his next lecture by adding a few more impressive Latin phrases. On his way back to the hotel, he decided to take a shortcut through an alley. The smell hit him first. Would the stench ruin his clothes?

He stepped over empty cans and bottles. Would his shoes be ruined? He saw a rat running in the shadows and then the figure of a man curled into a ball on the ground. It was a dirty man with a ragged scarf around his neck and a whiskey bottle at his feet. *This sight is repulsive*, he thought. His pace quickened as he pondered another Latin phrase for his lecture.

I offer this one: "*Hoc homo est hypocrita, hoc homo est hypocrita*!" Latin for "this man is a hypocrite." So much Latin, so little love.

Yet of the doctor and the alley-dweller, which is which? And who are we? Before you answer, consider this: "Pride goes before destruction, and a haughty spirit before a fall" (Proverbs 16:18). The doctor is sick with a raging fever of hypocrisy and arrogance, religion and self-importance. Aren't we all? Truth be told, wouldn't you rather sit with the doctor in a nice restaurant instead of with the drunk in a stinky alley? We are all sick with hypocrisy. The Great Physician, Jesus Christ, said, "Those who are well have no need of a physician, but those who are sick" (Matthew 9:12).

Let's take a walk, dear reader. We do not traverse a dark alley but a much worse place—a place of stench, a gruesome site of pain, agony, and death. Look at the three crosses on a hill. Look at the man on the cross in the center. He is one bloody mess from head to toe. Do you see His brow enthroned with thorn? the gouges in His hands and feet? the gashes in His body? Listen to the ugly shouts telling Him that if He is the Christ, then He should get down from the cross. Listen to the mocking tones of the soldiers.

Listen to Jesus say, "Father, forgive them . . ." (Luke 23:34).

This place reeks of suffering, sweat, blood, and death. Yet

above it all, the sweet aroma of the Savior's love is here. This is the place of Jesus and His love for the last, the least, and the lost—for each of us. Jesus walked to this place, not away from it. He never sidestepped this hill. He opened His holy hands for the nails. The beautiful Savior lovingly died for all of us ugly sinners upon the accursed cross. One Savior upon two beams of wood. There is no mask on His holy face, only bruises and blood. In this dark and gruesome place, we see the Savior's humility, love, compassion, and mercy.

May the mask of hypocrisy fall from our faces, for there is no need to wear it. There is no lower place than to look down on others. There is no greater theft than to take away hope in Christ. There is no one more foolish than the one who thinks he is wise. We are all filthy rags. The only great one is Christ.

Learn from the man in the alley. Make his prayer your own: "Lord, have mercy upon me, a sinner." Merciful Lord, grant this unto us all. Let us rejoice in the love of Christ, not ourselves or anyone else.

TREASURE: Recall the woman at the beginning of this chapter and the newcomer to Bible study. As the pastor, I said, "I thank God he has come here, to God's house," then explained in gentle words that all could hear, "The church is a place of truth, love, and mercy for all, a hospital for the sick, including you and me. Here the Great Physician binds our wounds and forgives our sins. The Lord rejoices that this man has come, just as He rejoices that you are here. If there is no hope for him, there is no hope for you, me, or any other human being. I will not tell him to leave, nor will anyone else. I pray you stay and welcome him to our midst."

It's easy to judge others, especially when they do things we would never think of doing. It's easy to hold ourselves above the riffraff and hide our sins in a deep, dark corner. Some sins become like the fabric of our lives. They are woven so intricately into our thinking that we are unable to distinguish them as sins. We are in the world but not of the world, after all. We would never embezzle from an employer or a charity. We would never be unfaithful to our spouse or abuse our child. But we might repeat a bit of gossip because it's too good not to share. We might cover up a mistake with a little white lie so we don't hurt someone else's feelings. We might cling to a grudge, too prideful to forgive the person who hurt us because we deserve better.

We read in Proverbs that "everyone who is arrogant in heart is an abomination to the Lord; be assured, he will not go unpunished" (Proverbs 16:5). Praise be to God that the punishment for our sin was taken to the cross. Our Redeemer poured out His blood for us so that the fabric of our lives is His robe of righteousness.

The woman who judged the newcomer to that Bible class understood my admonishment. She recognized her sin. Her contrition was visible to all in that class that day and was a reminder that Christ Jesus, who welcomed the tax collector to His side, welcomes us too.

Take Heart

Humility

If anyone says, "I love God," and hates his brother, he is a liar; for he who does not love his brother whom he has seen cannot love God whom he has not seen. (1 John 4:20)

And the Lord said: "Because this people draw near with their mouth and honor Me with their lips, while their hearts are far from Me, and their fear of Me is a commandment taught by men." (Isaiah 29:13)

Why do you see the speck that is in your brother's eye, but do not notice the log that is in your own eye? (Matthew 7:3)

Those who are well have no need of a physician, but those who are sick. Go and learn what this means: "I desire mercy, and not sacrifice." For I came not to call the righteous, but sinners. (Matthew 9:12–13)

God, be merciful to me, a sinner! (Luke 18:13)

Prayer

Loving Savior, Jesus Christ, forgive me for my hypocrisy, for thinking I am above others, for thinking my faith is greater, my gifts are more important, my steps are more secure. Forgive me for saying, "I'm glad I am not like that other person." How pharisaical I have been. Help me say with the tax collector, "God, be merciful to me, a sinner" (Luke 18:13). May I learn anew of Your humility, lavish love, and grace for me and all people. My I enter Your gates with thanksgiving. You alone are great. Amen.

CHAPTER 12

Truth

MY TROUBLE: False Doctrine

HIS TREASURE: Pure Truth

For pastors, teaching the great truths of God's Holy Word is a joy. His Word, a treasure we hold in our hands, is pure truth. Words concerning the Holy Bible, such as *inerrant* and *inspired*, should be familiar to each of us. Whoever and whatever contradicts the Bible is wrong. Jesus said, "If you abide in My word, you are truly My disciples, and you will know the truth, and the truth will set you free" (John 8:31–32). The truth sets before us Christ and the forgiveness, life, and salvation He has won for us in full. May we continue, remain, and abide in the treasure of His Holy Word!

TROUBLE: With this in mind, I ask you to look up Hezekiah 1:15. Write what you learn from that passage here: ____.
Please do the same for Psalm 151:7. Write what you learn from that passage here: ____.

I use this exercise with my eighth-grade confirmands and in some classes with adults as well. Every time I do, people look up the verses. You may have already recognized that the verses do not exist. This reveals a sad truth—we do not use our Bible often enough or know our Bible well enough to know immediately that those passages are nonexistent. Scriptural illiteracy leaves a vacuum that Satan and this fallen world eagerly fill with their foul and deadly lies. A vacuum is always filled.

Paul wrote to the congregation in Galatia, saying, "I am astonished that you are so quickly deserting Him who called you in the grace of Christ and are turning to a different gospel" (Galatians 1:6), adding later, "Who has bewitched you?" (Galatians 3:1). The Galatians had abandoned the truth of Christ and the gift of forgiveness for the lie of works righteousness that Satan set before them through deadly false teaching. The vacuum was filled with venomous lies as the serpent slithered in. False teaching binds people in chains of untruth and fear. Anything that is not Christ's Gospel is the devil's mantra. False teaching comes from hell and leads to hell. Here is an example: the saying "There is truth in all things" is an untruth. False teachers do not pray for others. They prey on them. Paul had corrective work to do: point the congregation back to Christ and to His pure truth. Souls were at stake. Souls are still at stake.

I think of Hazel. She did not reside in Galatia but in my own community. A modern false teacher had led her into darkness. (Praise God that she did not remain under his deadly tutelage.) When the truth of the Word of God exits, lies emerge.

Hazel was terrified. I saw fear in her eyes and heard it in her trembling voice. She showed me a letter she had received in the mail that brought her disturbing news: the Lord was going to curse her. She had been giving money to a televangelist who claimed that God would bless her monetarily with a "divine transfer" from the Lord. This "blessing" would be hers in only a matter of time! *What a blessing that would be*, she thought, a supplement to her sole source of income—social security benefits. She hadn't been feeling well. Perhaps the Lord will heal her too?

It is an interesting idea to give money in order to receive more money. This idea does not make *cents*. In fact, a bald-faced lie was being spoken into Hazel's ears. We should be aware when false teaching mentions money but does not mention God's mercy. Hazel was being robbed of her money month after month by a swindler, a wolf in sheep's clothing. She was being robbed of truth and comfort and was being terrorized by untruth.

This false teacher threatened her with a false curse because she had not sent money for a few months. Times were hard for her. Medical bills and utility bills had arrived in her mailbox, along with solicitations from the false teacher. Hazel feared that the only way to escape the curse was to start sending money again. That's the rhetoric of swindlers, but these are not words of the Lord.

Money is talked about far too much, and the riches of Christ are talked about far too little in so many circles. Television and the internet have opened channels for wolves, who have a ready audience to prey upon. Their teeth and claws sink into the lonely, the fearful, the burdened. These vulnerable souls are persuaded that God is a dispenser of money and that their lives will be enriched, someday, with a financial windfall. The wolves tell them that God may potentially bless them, and if He has not actually done so yet, then it means there is a hoop to jump through. If they keep putting cash and credit card numbers forward, God may do His part.

Note the language false teachers use. The misplaced focus is on the individual's actions. "*You* do this; *you* do that" to move the Lord's heart. The focus is on the potential monetary exchange between the individual and the Lord.

This is heartbreaking. Not only are Hazel and countless others robbed of creature comforts and trust in mankind, but they are also robbed of Christ and His Gospel as the riches of His pure love, grace, and mercy are not proclaimed by such swindlers.

The Bible says, "The love of money is a root of all kinds of evils" (1 Timothy 6:10). It also says, "Be content with what you have, for He has said "I will never leave you nor forsake you'" (Hebrews 13:5). Scanning the letter in my hands, I read the word *money* in every paragraph. "Send money, receive money." "If you send a bigger monetary pledge, then bigger bank blessings may come." It was all about cash, not Christ; all about lucre, not His love.

It was all . . . lies.

Then I saw in the last paragraph a word in bold: cursed. The letter told Hazel that if she sent money, the Lord *may* bless her. If she did not send money, God *would* curse her with disease, bankruptcy, mental illness, demons in her house, and other unspecified heartaches.

Hazel was terrified. "Pastor, I don't want to be cursed," she sobbed.

I had the high privilege of speaking the truth. "Hazel, be assured that you are not cursed, nor will you ever be. You are blessed, for the Lord loves you dearly and deeply. Blessed, for you are a baptized child of God and an heir of heaven. Blessed, for you are forgiven of your every sin. Jesus bled and died for you. You have the riches of His love and mercy always. You were bought with a price, the blood of Christ."

I took the letter from her hand and opened the Bible. "We know from God's Word that Jesus took the curse of our sin into His holy hands. He went to the cross, each step taken in pure love for you. His poverty yields riches for you in the form of His love, grace, mercy, forgiveness, and eternal life. Your salvation is not bought and sold by letters asking for your money. It is a free gift, given for you by Jesus' blood on the cross. Jesus Himself tells us, "So if the Son sets you free, you will be free indeed" (John 8:36).

For Hazel and us, pure and profound blessings are from the Lord, each one underserved, unearned, unmerited. There is no checking account or credit card numbers needed, no wallet, no withdrawals. There is no action we undertake to earn our salvation.

I placed Hazel's letter in the wastebasket where it belonged. I wrote to the sender and told him to stop tormenting this dear soul. The letters continued to arrive in her mailbox, but she never opened them again. She gave them to me.

Hazel died some years later, but for the remainder of her days on earth, she took heart because the truth of God's Word set her free from spiritual torment. The text for her funeral was Revelation 14:13: "Blessed are the dead who die in the Lord." She chose it herself. I am certain she did so with joy.

TREASURE: The truth God gives you in His Holy Word is

always available to you. Open your Bible and read it there for yourself. Be assured that by the faith given to you by the Holy Spirit, you may rejoice in the truth of the Savior's love for you!

Take Heart

Pure Truth

All Scripture is breathed out by God and profitable for teaching, for reproof, for correction, and for training in righteousness. (2 Timothy 3:16)

Your word is truth. (John 17:17)

Blessed rather are those who hear the word of God and keep it! (Luke 11:28)

These are written so that you may believe that Jesus is the Christ, the Son of God, and that by believing you may have life in His name. (John 20:31)

No prophecy was ever produced by the will of man, but men spoke from God as they were carried along by the Holy Spirit. (2 Peter 1:21)

Prayer

Heavenly Father, I joyfully say with the psalmist, "The sum of Your word is truth, and every one of Your righteous rules endure forever" (Psalm 119:160). How blessed I am to read, hear, mark, learn, and take to heart Your Holy Word. I praise You, for Your Word declares me forgiven, loved, your child, an heir of heaven. In Jesus' name. Amen.

CHAPTER 13

Hope

MY TROUBLE: Depression

HIS TREASURE: Hope

TROUBLE: What comes to mind when someone invites you to go with them to a nursing home? Hesitation, perhaps, because of the reminder of your mortality? Or sadness because residents are no longer able to do what they had once done? You may even recoil. After all, the frailties of the human body are unavoidable.

It won't surprise you that, as a pastor, I often visit people in nursing homes. It's part of my job to read Scripture with them, pray with them, administer the Sacrament. We might sing a hymn or tell each other stories. And it might be a reasonable conclusion that such visits are depressing. But don't reach that conclusion just yet.

One of the people I visit on a regular basis is a forty-four-year-old woman who has lived in a nursing home for seven years. Her diagnosis of multiple sclerosis brought with it a devastating reality of loss. For in time, she lost her mobility, her job, her husband, and more.

Multiple sclerosis is an unpredictable and unforgiving disease. This once vibrant, athletic young woman could no longer move her arms or legs. She loved to ride horses, but that has been taken away. Swallowing is a struggle, and her voice is faint. I must bend down and listen closely and carefully to hear her faint voice. Her arms and legs are so very thin. She cannot comb her hair or brush her teeth. She says the same thing to me every time I visit, month after month, year after year.

How would you respond to someone who asked if you are upbeat and happy all the time? I was asked that in Bible class not long ago. Some people were surprised when I said no. I am not always happy. Life is difficult for parishioners and pastors alike. Some situations never improve, and the knowledge that this is as good as it gets is hard to bear, even for pastors. The Bible records more than once that Jesus wept. The Bible speaks of people being downcast and of dark thoughts. Are *you* always upbeat and joyous?

Of course not. In fact, you may feel empty and utterly alone. You may believe that no one in this whole wide world cares about you—not a single person among your family, not one of your neighbors or even a stranger. They say empty words that deliver nothing of substance, platitudes that are painful to hear. "Exercise more." "Eat better." "You just need more faith." "Pray more." "God doesn't give you anything you can't handle." "Oh, don't feel bad." These tidbits of advice do nothing to assuage your mind. You are left alone and want to scream, "But I *do* feel bad. Do you hear what I'm saying? Does anyone care?"

Unsolicited advice is readily given, but it does nothing to

soothe your gaping wounds. Some people listen briefly, try to fix you, then move on. Some don't lend an ear or a hand at all. The wounds you carry are not visible to others; no bandage can cover them, and no cream can soothe them. But you hurt deep down to your core. You feel empty and alone, even in a crowd, even with friends, even with family. One more tear falls. You sigh and want to pull the covers over your head and stay in bed. Your life is a living hell. You say again, "But I *do* feel bad. Do you hear what I'm saying? Does anyone care?"

It may help to know that despite the feelings of isolation and despair, you are not alone. There were others who knew this similitude of darkness, this deep pain from within. Look in the Bible for proof. David wrote, "I have been forgotten like one who is dead; I have become like a broken vessel" (Psalm 31:12). Heman lamented, "You have put me in the depths of the pit, in the regions dark and deep" (Psalm 88:6). Jonah cried, "Therefore now, O Lord, please take my life from me, for it is better for me to die than to live" (Jonah 4:3). Job asked, "Why did I not die at birth, come out from the womb and expire?" (Job 3:11). Elijah bemoaned, "It is enough; now, O Lord, take away my life, for I am no better than my fathers" (1 Kings 19:4).

You are not alone.

On a family vacation when I was about ten years old, I walked through a cemetery that was near our hotel. The memory is vivid to this moment. I saw a name on a weathered stone: "Greta." No date of birth or death were listed. No last name. But these words were etched on the stone: "Loved but was loved not. Died as she lived—alone." Greta—what happened? Did you wander in darkness your whole life? Were you deeply wounded, wondering as you lived and died if anyone loved you? Was hope buried for you long before your body was laid in the grave? Who chose the words for your headstone, epitomizing your life this way?

Perhaps you feel as though you are walking in Greta's footsteps. Perhaps her epitaph evokes thoughts of a descriptive summary of your own life. Would your life be descried as dark, worthless, lonely?

It can be difficult to see through the feelings of worthlessness and defeat, but know this for certain: there is One who truly understands how you feel and what you are facing, and He cares for you deeply. Jesus Christ, our Lord, knew ridicule and mockery, for "they were striking His head with a reed and spitting on Him" (Mark 15:19). He knew the depths of grief, for He Himself said, "My soul is very sorrowful, even to death" (Matthew 26:38). He knew rejection, for "many of His disciples turned back and no longer walked with Him" (John 6:66). He knew what it was to be utterly forsaken as He cried out, "My God, My God, why have You forsaken Me?" (Matthew 27:46).

Jesus, true man, felt every terrible feeling we can feel. He knows what we're experiencing. But there is more. Jesus, true God, loves you. Jesus is your refuge, a mighty beacon of hope in all circumstances. The Lord assures you that He "will satisfy the weary soul, and every languishing soul I will replenish" (Jeremiah 31:25). Jesus gave His back to the whip for you, but He will never turn His back on you. He was forsaken, but He will never forsake you. His hand was pierced for you, but He will not let you slip through His fingers. Ever. Cast your every burden upon Him. He is there for you. Always.

Dark thoughts can come into our minds. Christians are not always cheerful. The Bible speaks of trials and burdens for all of us. Life presents struggles. Situations may depress us. Challenges can seem overwhelming. We wonder if anyone cares. When darkness encroaches upon us, and it certainly will, one shining truth calms and comforts us: we are loved by Christ. Knowing that single truth overcomes a multitude of dark thoughts—every single one, every single time. This does not mean we will jump with happiness, smile, and whistle all day, every day. What does this mean, then? When we are weak, Jesus is our strength. When we stand in the shadows of pain, the light of His love brightens the darkness. He is with you, and you can cast every burden upon Him.

If I could speak with Greta, I would tell her that the epitaph on her gravestone is wrong. The words "was loved not" are unfitting for her, for everyone. I would erase the first and last words on Greta's stone until just one word remains, and that word is fitting for Greta and us: *loved.*

The father of lies and our own sinful nature can take us to very dark places, but this is never to be equated with a weak faith. No, this is life in a fallen world. Despite this, we can all take heart because we have Jesus Christ, the light of the world. The brilliant rays of His love shine in the darkness and envelop you. He sees you. He lifts you from the slimy pit and carries you in His strong arms. He cares for you. And He loves you earnestly and eternally.

TREASURE: Think back to the young woman we met at the beginning of this chapter. When I visit her in the nursing home, I lean in and listen carefully, and I am uplifted. She always speaks of hope and comfort in Christ. Through years of visits, I have watched her wither physically. Her mobility is gone. Her strength is gone. Her husband, horse, and house are gone. Yet she has hope, rich and full. She never complains about her life or speaks of what she has lost. Instead, she speaks of what she has in Christ: love, mercy, hope, forgiveness, peace, eternal life. She is an example to me that even in unpleasant circumstances we can give praise to God and point others to Him. I hope she is for you too.

Listen closely to her. Let her uplift you. Take heart.

Take Heart

Hope

I waited patiently for the Lord; He inclined to me and heard my cry. He drew me up from the pit of destruction, out of the miry bog, and set my feet upon a rock, making my steps secure. (Psalm 40:1–2)

The Lord is near to the brokenhearted and saves the crushed spirit. (Psalm 34:18)

Why are you cast down, O my soul, and why are you in turmoil within me? Hope in God; for I shall again praise Him, my salvation and my God. (Psalm 42:11)

In my distress I called upon the LORD; to my God I cried for help. From His temple He heard my voice, and my cry to Him reached His ears. (Psalm 18:6)

Humble yourselves, therefore, under the mighty hand of God so that at the proper time He may exalt you, casting all your anxieties on Him, because He cares for you. (1 Peter 5:6–7)

Prayer

Gracious Lord, at times, I think no one cares for me, that I am all alone. These thoughts are too much for me. I am weary. Yet I know that You hear my plea for comfort. I cast my burdens upon You, merciful Savior, as You so lovingly bid me. You wept, and You know exactly what I am thinking, feeling, and facing. You are my rest, refuge, and rock. Help me. In Your holy name. Amen.

CHAPTER 14

The Resurrection

MY TROUBLE(S): Death and Grief

HIS TREASURE: The Obituary of Death

TROUBLE: I waited in the hospital hallway. This is a most difficult situation—I have to tell a wife that her husband of two years has died. All she knows is that he was brought to the hospital after a car accident. The accident did not take place as a result of a car moving at a high rate of speed on a highway. No one was even driving. He was using a torch under the car, and suddenly there was an explosion of flames, and he burned to death. She is running down the hallway now. Police officers escort her to me. What will I say?

To love others hurts deeply. This is because life is fragile, and those we love are with us for a limited time. Simply put but profoundly true is that those dear to us are on loan from the Lord. Please do not wait until tomorrow to express your love to others. Put this book down and seize the opportunity now. Our time with others is temporary. Death shatters the family circle, leaving our hearts in countless pieces. Our lives are now like puzzle pieces all over the floor. Who can put them together again? Our lives will never be the same. Never. Ever. We are left to hold our departed loved ones close in memory and cherish the time the Lord allotted us with them. Yet there is so much more.

To love hurts. How do I know? From pastoral experience. I have seen this in the faces and heard it in the voices of those under my care for nearly four decades. I have officiated at funerals for people of all ages, infants to the advanced elderly, comforting the sorrowing with the precious salve of God's Holy Word. The sorrow and pain that death brings to others—the tears, groans, sobs—following the death of a loved one is a pain to be acknowledged and not ignored.

To love hurts. How do I know? From personal experience. My mother died after a massive heart attack. My father died from cancer. My sister was murdered on 9/11. She was a passenger aboard American Airlines flight 77. My brother died from complications associated with alcoholism. Our child was stillborn. My brother-in-law died by suicide. Family members, good friends, congregants, childhood friends. The old and the young. The rich and the poor. The well-known and unknown. The list is long, and it continually grows name by name. Dead, dead, dead.

Tears, groans, utter heartache, yours and mine. We seek healing in books, with grief counselors, and over time. But we still live with grief and will do so until the moment we die. It's ironic that we all live with death. Yet there is so much more to this life, and we can take heart because we have Jesus, our loving, living, and triumphant Savior. It is His love that heals.

Jesus Christ, the living Lord, alone can dress the deep, grievous, and gaping wounds of a broken heart. The birth registry in Bethlehem leads to a death certificate in Jerusalem. He laid His perfect life down on the cross for you—the sinless for the sinful. He faced death head-on, willingly hung suspended between the earth He created and the heavenly abode He left in order to rescue and redeem fallen humanity. The death of Christ is always coupled with His bodily resurrection. He never taught one without the other.

From the cross, and only from the cross, our Savior said, "It is finished" (John 19:30). Not after He tread the waves, fed the hungry multitudes, gave sight to people who were blind and mobility to people who couldn't walk did Jesus say, "Finished." This cry of victory from holy parched, cracked, and bloody lips is reserved for one place: the cross. It's a cry of victory, not of defeat; it's a loud cry, not a faint whimper. "Finished!" The work of our salvation was paid in full with the sweat, blood, and life of God's only Son. Jesus laid down His life. Lifeless and still, the light of the world is placed in the dark borrowed tomb. Jesus was in the throat of death and then swallowed. Silence, deafening silence, for three days.

On the third day, the Easter trumpet resounded clearly and the silence was forever broken! The joyous proclamation is clear with sweet tones of victory: "He is risen!" The Easter banner is forever unfurled! The angelic choirs break in with a beautiful anthem of life—He lives! He lives, who once was dead. The borrowed tomb is empty. Jesus lives! He is risen bodily, mightily, victoriously. Drop the spices! From the tomb wafts the sweet aroma of life, not the stench of death. The empty tomb fills us with eternal comfort. The greatest news comes from a cemetery! Jesus lives! The gloating of death and the grave are gagged forever.

Come, see the place where they laid Him. See the burial cloths, the head wrapping. See the angels. Hear the angels: "He has risen; He is not here. See the place where they laid Him" (Mark 16:6). Rejoice, for death is dead. Sorrow sorrows. The grave groans. The death certificate for death is signed, sealed, and delivered with the blood of Jesus Christ, the living one. Jesus has won the victory fully and forever over sin, death, and hell—the obituary for death! Two words change everything right now and for all eternity for us: "Jesus lives." Oh, the comfort!

Jesus lives. How does this historical truth assuage our grief? He lives. Therefore, we are never alone. *You* are never alone. Jesus lives, and He dresses your deepest wounds with the precious salve of His Word and Holy Sacraments. Jesus lives, and He hears your every sigh and groan. He knows your sorrows, for He wept as He stood before the tomb of Lazarus. He loves *you*.

Please note that we are comforted in the midst of our sorrows, not cured. Our grief ebbs and flows, while Christ's love for us is steady, strong, and unwavering. We are comforted in our sorrow because we know that those who have gone before us in the true and saving faith are with the Lord. "My desire is to depart and be with Christ, for that is far better," Paul said (Philippians 1:23).

Jesus assured the thief on the cross, "Today you will be with Me in paradise" (Luke 23:43), and He proclaims the same promise to us. "Let not your hearts be troubled," He says. "Believe in God; believe also in Me. In My Father's house are many rooms. If it were not so, would I have told you that I go to prepare a place for you? And if I go and prepare a place for you, I will come again and will take you to Myself, that where I am you may be also" (John 14:1–3). My mother is home, by the grace of our Savior. Dad—home by grace. Little one—home by grace. Sister, brother, brother-in-law—home by grace. Your loved one is standing in heavenly splendor before the Lord and hearing the triumphant heavenly anthem. "Salvation belongs to our God who sits on the throne, and to the Lamb!" (Revelation 7:10). Look and listen. What a sight! What a sound! The love of our Lord and Savior, Jesus, sees us through this vale of tears and will see us safely home, just as He promised.

A grand reunion is coming for us. We will be reunited with those who have departed in the true and saving faith. Not now, but then. Not here, but there, in the heavenly mansions. Thank God for the time we had with them and for the memories that were made together. Look back and remember, dear friend. Embrace the memories. Look around you, dear friend. Your front and rear guard is Jesus. Look ahead, dear friend, to the time when you will be reunited with those dear to you. Your separation is temporary; your reunion everlasting. Comfort is yours as you look ahead, for your last earthly breath yields to heavenly joy. A deep dark grave is not your future. The light and glory of heaven is. Our heavenly homeland is assured. We may not be able to speak of an easy life, but we can certainly speak of eternal life.

Our bodies will rest in a grave, but the grave is a temporary chamber for our bodies. One day, our grave will be empty. Jesus will return on the Last Day in all His glory, and He will say, "Arise! Come out!" Sown in weakness and dishonor, our bodies will be raised in strength and glory. Then we will be with the Lord for eternity. Thus, we confess in the Apostles' Creed, "I believe in . . . the forgiveness of sins, the resurrection of the body, and the life everlasting. Amen." This is a most comforting truth!

The Lord has taken care of everything as we live and as we die. He sees everything with eyes of mercy and compassion. Grief impacts us emotionally, physically, socially, and spiritually, but it is tempered with hope. Although our lives will never be the same when our family circle is shattered, we can be confident that Jesus "is the same yesterday and today and forever" (Hebrews 13:8). We will live with this heartache throughout our earthly life. Our grief will be acute and then lessen, intensify, and abate. We will not "get over it," but we will be comforted through it by Jesus, who tirelessly and unfailingly sustains us with His Word of mercy, compassion, understanding, and love. We are not comfortless; we are comforted. We are not hopeless; we are hopeful. Let us take heart! We have Christ, and two words concerning Him change everything today, tomorrow, and for all eternity for each of us: Jesus lives.

TREASURE: (Please bear with me.) Recall the young woman mentioned at the chapter's beginning. At the words "Chris died," she fell into my arms and sobbed. Her beloved husband was only twenty-two years old. He had so much life left to live, or so he had thought. She said something then I have never forgotten: "I am thankful that I told him I loved him this morning before I left. He stood in the garage waving as I drove away." The risen Lord tended to her grieving heart through Word and Sacrament, and He continues to do so to this very moment.

What of those who do not have the sweet memory of speaking loving words to a loved one for the last time? What of those whose parting words were careless or selfish? Countless people have said to me, "I wish." I wish I had said I loved her. I wish I had hugged him one more time. I wish I had one more hour with them. Grief can give rise to regret.

But Jesus and His word of eternal life had the final say, not death's ghastly voice. Let us love today, and may we be comforted each day with the truth that Jesus lives. Oh, the comfort! This is a treasure indeed.

Take Heart

The Obituary of Death

Yes, we are of good courage, and we would rather be away from the body and at home with the Lord. (2 Corinthians 5:8)

You guide me with Your counsel, and afterward You will receive me to glory. (Psalm 73:24)

I am the resurrection and the life. Whoever believes in Me, though he die, yet shall he live, and everyone who lives and believes in Me shall never die. (John 11:25–26)

He will swallow up death forever; and the Lord GOD will wipe away tears from all faces. (Isaiah 25:8)

And after my skin has been thus destroyed, yet in my flesh I shall see God, whom I shall see for myself, and my eyes shall behold, and not another. My heart faints within me! (Job 19:26–27)

Prayer

Risen Savior, You laid down Your life for me and took it up again on the third day with Your bodily resurrection. Mortal life is fragile, but Your promises are unbreakable. Remind me of the truth that You defeated death and that heaven is my home by Your grace. May I rejoice that Your love sees me safely home. Comfort me with the promise of a joyous reunion with those who have gone before me in the true and saving faith that awaits me when I breathe my last. May I take comfort in the familiar words of the creed: "The forgiveness of sins, the resurrection of body, and the life everlasting." Comfort abounds, for You live, now and forever. Amen.

CHAPTER 15

Mercy

MY TROUBLE: Anger

HIS TREASURE: Long-Suffering Mercy

TROUBLE: It was a regularly scheduled voters meeting, and the pastor, who was present, didn't anticipate any problems. After he gave his report, board members down the line gave theirs—the elders, the treasurer, the education chair, and so on. There was no old business to report. So far, so good. "Is there any new business?" the president of the congregation asked.

"Yes," a man said immediately. "I move that pastor's . . ."

Now on full alert, the pastor held his breath.

"Do not let the sun go down on your anger, and give no opportunity to the devil" (Ephesians 4:26–27). The sad truth is that we all have given Satan opportunity. The sun has risen and set repeatedly on our anger. We cultivate grudges day after day and night after night. We have called down God's anger upon others—those we know well and those we do not know. Minutes, hours, days, weeks, months, and years come and go. All the while, we carefully marinate and carefully stir the smelly stew of our anger. It is a sure recipe for disaster.

Haven't we all given a foothold to the devil? Our grudges rise quickly, and our simmering anger eventually boils over. "Be angry and do not sin" (Ephesians 4:26). We are angry as we drive, as we shop, in our homes, on social media, at the television, at others, at ourselves. We go to bed mad and get up mad. Hot heads and cold hearts. If looks could kill—we glare and frown at others. Anger has gotten the best of us at dawn, through the day, and at dusk.

Anger is one of the emotions the Lord gave us. But how we handle anger may become a problem. Bloodless murder is murder nonetheless when it takes the form of "I wish you were dead" thoughts. We can mask our anger with our smiles, but it remains. Anger is acidic as it eats away at us and our relationships. Who are you upset with? What took place that has upset you? Fill in the blanks: I am angry at ____________________ because of __________________________. (How many more spaces do you need?)

Something may have happened yesterday or years ago that upset you. Why are you letting that situation dictate your thoughts and feelings today? Your anger may be directed at a clerk you met just once in a store. You determined he was rude to you. Someone at church snubbed you, and you can't let it go. Someone cut you off while you were driving to work, and you laid on the horn and then made an obscene gesture. Classy. Your sibling upset you with a rude comment, and you let him have it.

You play the scenario of getting even over and over in your

mind. Your blood pressure rises. Your brow is furrowed. Your face turns red. Your heart pounds. Acidic anger. You think of ways to tell off the person who angered you. The whole pot of anger stew is dumped down his or her throat, and it's scalding hot to boot. Make that person pay.

We have short fuses, and they are lit. Anger blows up relationships and friendships. The shrapnel of anger wounds and injures others. Read the following examples:

The wife in tears whose husband spat angrily and abusively in her face.

The daughter whose mother daily berates her for being "stupid, fat, and lazy."

The third grader who drew his family, putting a scowl on his father's face. "He's always mad," the young artist stated.

The pastor criticizing his members as "dumb."

The obscene gesture a teacher flashed to her slow-driving neighbor as she passed him on the highway.

The organist practicing "Joy to the World" exploded in a tirade because people were talking in the sanctuary.

The man upset because the church service was too long. How could pastor not know the first Nation-

al Football League games of the season were on at noon?

The woman angry because people at church weren't friendly enough. She left the service pouting and never came back.

The man furious at his neighbor who accidentally mowed a foot over the lot line.

The woman mad because her sister always talked about her own children and never asked about her nieces and nephews.

The couple in marriage counseling because the husband said something his wife did not like—twenty-five years earlier.

This list could go on for pages. And what about you? What is simmering on your stove? I ask myself the same question. Has my anger boiled over and made a smelly mess?

Anger can be well-placed in certain situations, including anger at injustice, poverty, and greed. The Bible records Jesus' righteous anger when He saw that the temple courtyard was being used as a marketplace (see Matthew 21:12–17 and John 2:13–17). Perhaps we should be the angriest at ourselves for hurting others, for making excuses for our cold hearts and hot heads, for being short on patience. Our explosive outbursts directed at people we know well or hardly know at all add to the simmering pot of anger stew. Our smoldering rage causes us to act like spoiled children throwing tantrums, putting people in their place, and destroying relationships. We keep a record of wrongs done to us but seldom of what we have done to others.

Things happen to all of us that we can use to excuse our anger. What do we do then? Forgive. Paul tells us to "be kind to one another, tenderhearted, forgiving one another, as God in Christ forgave you" (Ephesians 4:32). Daily, we ask our heavenly Father to "forgive us our trespasses as we forgive those who trespass against us."

The sun rises and sets every day. You can allow the first streaks of dawn and the last light of the evening to leave you feeling angry. You can greet another morning seething, plotting revenge, wasting the day with angry thoughts and tossing and turning all night. Or, with the help of Christ, you can break this destructive pattern Satan delights in.

Christ is here for you with His grace, mercy, compassion, and forgiveness. "Create in me a clean heart, O God, and renew a right spirit with me" (Psalm 51:10). The divine surgeon takes out your heart of stone and replaces it with a heart of flesh. He writes your prescription in His own rich, red blood: "Forgiven in full." Cast your burden of anger upon Him and let His refreshing baptismal water satisfy your soul. The gift of His peace that passes all understanding is given freely to you. The sweet aroma of forgiveness wipes out the stench of anger. The sun rises, the sun sets—that pattern is sure—but it need no longer do so on your anger. Take heart! The Lord grants you a new day. His mercies are new each and every morning! Thanks be to God! You are given the free and abundant gift of forgiveness in the cross of Christ, and now you can give that same gift to others.

TREASURE: Recall the voters meeting and the new business regarding the pastor. A motion was made and quickly seconded to reduce his salary by five thousand dollars a year. There was no discussion, and the vote passed. Why? Some people were angry at their pastor because he rightly said a rock-and-roll piece was not suited for the Divine Service, that the secular didn't belong with the sacred music of the worship service. Some voters wanted to hurt him by reducing his salary. They had concocted their plans weeks before and eagerly awaited the quarterly meeting to see them come to fruition. All went according to plan, and they grabbed the pastor's throat by cutting his salary—an angry, hurtful message. Ugly, angry meetings take place in congregations regularly. What must the Lord think?

Where is the treasure in this? It is here: other members of the congregation had a different plan. They passed the hat and raised more than double what was taken away. There was no motion, no second, no discussion, and no vote. That afternoon, the anonymous gift was placed in the pastor's mailbox. He never learned who did this.

The treasure is the beauty of such kindness that motivates us to seek to do good as a response to the goodness our Lord does for us every day, an acknowledgment of the provision He bestows, and a generous spirit that shares the grace of our Lord Jesus. God be praised!

Take Heart

Long-Suffering Mercy

Put on then, as God's chosen ones, holy and beloved, compassionate hearts, kindness, humility, meekness, and patience, bearing with one another and, if one has a complaint against another, forgiving each other; as the Lord has forgiven you, so you also must forgive. (Colossians 3:12–13)

Beloved, let us love one another, for love is from God, and whoever loves has been born of God and knows God. (1 John 4:7)

And whenever you stand praying, forgive, if you have anything against anyone, so that your Father also who is in heaven may forgive you your trespasses. (Mark 11:25)

Better is a dry morsel with quiet than a house full of feasting with strife. (Proverbs 17:1)

A soft answer turns away wrath, but a harsh word stirs up anger. (Proverbs 15:1)

Prayer

Merciful Father, forgive me for being angry with others, including those in my own family, those in my congregation, and even those on the street. I have kept a record of wrongs. I have given a wide and strong foothold to Satan. Lord, have mercy upon me. The sun rises and sets upon Your unchanging love for me in Christ, Your Son, my Lord. Grant me the gift of forgiveness. Help me readily forgive others. Grant me patience with others and a kind heart toward them. May all be to Your glory. In Jesus' name. Amen.

CHAPTER 16

Contentment

MY TROUBLE: Envy

HIS TREASURE: Contentment

TROUBLE: I felt greatly discontented. In truth, it's more accurate to say that I was envious, petty, and jealous. I was just out of seminary and assigned to be an assistant pastor. I didn't want to be an assistant pastor. I wondered why the Lord would have done this to me. I deserved better than this, right? In my circuit, there was a seasoned senior pastor whose congregation dwarfed mine three times over. Attendance there was five times higher than that of my congregation. *This guy has it all*, I thought. And he said as much. He was going to be the next speaker for *The Lutheran Hour*. If not that, then at least a district president. His sermons, according to his own assessment, were riveting, and his thunderous voice commanded attention. He commented on how hard he worked, which was harder than all the other pastors in the circuit, district, and even the Synod. He stood in the spotlight with confidence. I couldn't help but compare myself to him, and as I did, discontent dragged me into the dark shadows of envy where it is difficult to see God's blessings. I felt that I was so much less than him. Comparison robs us of contentment.

Paul penned that he was content, whatever state he was in, whatever was going on in his life (Philippians 4:11). His contentment did not rest with his circumstances but with Christ. He wrote that "godliness with contentment is great gain, for we brought nothing into the world, and we cannot take anything out of the world" (1 Timothy 6:6–7). What a gift to be content with ourselves and with any circumstance that comes our way. What a gift to have contentment in the midst of trial and trouble, knowing the Lord will take care of us, or contentment with self and not competition with others, knowing we are uniquely created by a loving God. But in a world broken by sin, we are burdened by the lie that we fall woefully short and content with our discontent.

You and I both know people who are unhappy with their body, their job, their circumstances. The more they compare themselves to others, the more discontent they feel. Their self-talk may sound like this: "There he is with his muscles. Show off. Why does he always wear those short-sleeve shirts anyway?" "There she is with another fancy new dress. Who does she think she is—a model? Her figure isn't that great." "They offered to pay for my meal again, always waving their cash in my face. Braggarts." "He always raises his hand in class, acting so smart." Rooted in feelings of inadequacy and inferiority, envy consists of comparison and competition. Envy says, "The spotlight should always be on me, and never you. The stage is mine, and mine alone. So move along."

Here we are with our envious thoughts. We frown at the successful among us and smile when someone falters. We want what others have and hold ourselves superior when they lack. We compete and compare, over and over again. The problem, though, is not with what other people have and do; it is with how we perceive and respond. On a hot day, the man simply wore a short-sleeve shirt. The woman had worked hard and bought a new dress with her earnings; it's that simple. They are a generous couple and paid for a friend's meal. This is not about a shirt, a dress, some money—it is about envy.

What are the origins of envy? The answer is simple—it begins in our own sinful heart. We hear the evil one's lie that we are lacking. Someone else is more attractive, stronger, wealthier, smarter. Someone else has newer, nicer, better things. Someone else has a bigger congregation and preaches better sermons. To compare ourselves with others and to compete with them is the sure recipe for a bitter batch of envy. Comparison robs us of joy and feeds our never-satisfied appetite of inferiority.

Consider the following:

Joseph's brothers put his dreams in a bad light, which led them to conspire: "Come now, let us kill him and throw him into one of the pits" (Genesis 37:20).

King Ahab envied Naboth's vineyard and was unhappy when he was denied it. Ahab "lay down on his bed and turned away his face and would eat no food" (1 Kings 21:4). He wore a crown of childishness.

Rachel envied her sister Leah: "When Rachel saw

that she bore Jacob no children, she envied her sister. She said to Jacob, 'Give me children, or I shall die!'" (Genesis 30:1).

King Saul envied David after Goliath had been slain: "The women sang to one another as they celebrated, 'Saul has struck down his thousands, and David his ten thousands.' And Saul was very angry, and this saying displeased him" (1 Samuel 18:7–8).

There are other biblical examples of envy, but let this passage suffice in summary: "A tranquil heart gives life to the flesh, but envy makes the bones rot" (Proverbs 14:30). Read the verse again. Envy is rottenness. It is a gnawing parasite on the inside, a raging fever of constant vexation that produces foul thought: "I need to have what you have; I need it for me; I need it now." Envy destroys you by eating away at you from the inside out. It is the thief of joy and the murderer of contentment.

Ponder these questions:

Will your whole life be lived comparing yourself to others?

Why do you compare yourself to others?

What good has envy done for you in the past?

What good will envy ever do for you?

Why are you threatened by others?

Have you had enough? "Lord, I confess my sin of envy and

the rottenness that lodges in my heart. Forgive me for my envy and petty jealousy. Forgive me for saying by my actions and in my thoughts that You have shortchanged me. Forgive me for my envious vocabulary. I've had enough, Lord. Forgive me. Help me. In Jesus' name. Amen."

Confession brings with it refreshment. The Lord is profuse with His forgiveness and mercy. He delights in comforting you. Stop comparing yourself to others. There is no need. The Lord created you and redeemed you. You are not less than or better than others. You are loved by Him. In His wisdom and according to His plan for you and those around you, your heavenly Father placed you where you are. By His grace, you have all you really need. Keep this great scriptural truth, a humbling truth, front and center as you live your daily life: "If we confess our sins, He is faithful and just to forgive us our sins and to cleanse us from all unrighteousness" (1 John 1:9).

Our Lord Jesus—true God from all eternity and true man, born in our flesh for our sake—provides abundantly all we need. Great and absolute are His gifts of love, mercy, grace, and forgiveness. Jesus was not content to let you perish in your sin. He was not content to let you suffer without hope through this earthly life. Instead, He gave His life in exchange for yours. Now, you, an heir of the Most High God, will receive all the lavish, endless, glorious gifts of heaven.

Armed with this truth, you can say to the man who is in better physical shape than you, "Nice shirt, my friend." You can tell the woman with the dress, "That looks nice on you." You can say to the people who paid for your meal, "Thank you for your kindness. It'll be my treat next time." Or you don't have to say anything.

How different from before! Nothing has changed in these people, but you have changed. You have a new perspective, a clear focus. Your contentment is rooted in the peace Christ gives you. Because His peace is yours, by the Holy Spirit, you now have peace with yourself and can share that peace with others. You can have an appreciation for what the Lord blesses you with and can appreciate the gifts He bestows to others. Contentment, not comparison. Encouragement for others, not discouragement. This is a much better way to live and has no heavy baggage tagged "envy" to lug along. Believe me; envy proves too heavy a load.

A wise seminary classmate said to me bluntly all those years ago, "What's your problem? Why are you so jealous? Why are you so discontented with where the Lord placed you to serve? Why are you comparing yourself to other pastors? That's petty. Who are you trying to impress, and why? They aren't the problem. You are." Ouch! He was right.

TREASURE: Comparison is the thief of joy. Envy demeans only the one who is envious. Jealousy brings nothing but heartache. Discontentment makes the Lord petty and small. Let go of envy. Repent.

This can be difficult, particularly when negative thoughts have become habitual. But turn your mind to the blessings God has provided you, to the abundant gifts of the Spirit. Ask God to help you see the treasures He lays before you. Namely this: Jesus was not content to let you die in your sin. Our obedient, loving Lord was the complete and final fulfillment of God's Law. He spilled His holy blood for you, died in your stead, and rose again so that you will have eternal life. Take heart! Contentment is yours in Christ. For in Him, you lack nothing and have everything.

Take Heart

Contentment

For where jealousy and selfish ambition exist, there will be disorder and every evil practice. (James 3:16)

You desire and do not have, so you murder. You covet and cannot obtain, so you fight and quarrel. You do not have, because you do not ask. (James 4:2)

Love is patient and kind; love does not envy or boast; it is not arrogant. (1 Corinthians 13:4)

For the sake of Christ, then, I am content with weaknesses, insults, hardships, persecutions, and calamities. For when I am weak, then I am strong. (2 Corinthians 12:10)

Keep your life free from love of money, and be content with what you have, for He has said, "I will never leave you nor forsake you." (Hebrews 13:5)

Prayer

Most loving Savior, forgive me for my own petty jealousy and sinful envy. Grant me a repentant heart. May I rejoice in You and Your love for me. May I also rejoice in the blessings You bestow upon others. In Your holy name. Amen.

CHAPTER 17

Past, Present, Future in His Loving Hands

MY TROUBLE: My Past, Present, and Future

HIS TREASURE: An Assured Past, Present, and Future

TROUBLE: How would you fill in these blanks:

What troubles me about my past is ______________________________

______________________________.

What troubles me about my present is ______________________________

______________________________.

What troubles me about my future is ______________________________

______________________________.

Everyone has a past. Some have skeletons rattling in the far corners of their closet. We may speak of the past as dark, checkered, shady, questionable. We remember things we did in days long gone that no one else knows about. The recollection is vivid: that lie you told, that angry gesture, that silly argument. Maybe you remember a friendship that was once strong but now is weak beyond repair. Perhaps there were lustful thoughts; perhaps the skeleton in your closet is an infidelity. God knows all this about you.

The past impacts the present. We can talk with ease about events that affected world history and still shape the present. But we are reticent to speak of our own history, our past misdeeds, mistakes, and mishaps that shape our present. We may privately ruminate with regret over our past. What does this avail us?

Are you troubled by your past, by an event, by a person, by your actions, by a poor decision? I am. The trip down memory lane is painful to navigate with its ditches, ravines, and steep slopes. Your past might infect your present and cause you to wonder if God will forgive *that* sin. Take heart—right now—and remember one word that covers your past and mine: *forgiven*. An impactful word for this very moment, forgiveness is a full, free gift. We are not chained to or jailed by our past actions. The cell door is not slammed shut and forever locked, leaving us to languish in a dark corner. The comfort for our conscience is Christ.

Your heavenly Father declares you righteous, freeing you from your past. We live in the forgiveness of our sins. This very moment is marked with grace and mercy for you. Treasure this truth right now: "I, I am He who blots out your transgressions for My own sake, and I will not remember your sins" (Isaiah 43:25). The all-knowing God forgives and forgets your every sin! He placed them all on His Son, Jesus Christ, the "Lamb of God, who takes away the sin of the world!" (John 1:29). The Lamb's sacrifice removed your sin with His holy blood. Your troubled past is your forgiven past. The skeletons rattling in the closet are replaced by a flesh-and-blood, risen Savior who delights in pronouncing "Forgiven" into your ears. Case closed. Verdict rendered. Pardon extended. Our past is best summarized by one word, by one name: *Christ*. Our past is forgotten—but we never are. Your name and mine are carved on the hand of Jesus—right by the nail mark. Forgive yourself, for the Lord has forgiven you.

"Well and good concerning my past," you retort, "but what about my present life? I have so many challenges and problems. The current days are so troubling for me!" Be assured that today's troubles are acknowledged by our omniscient God. We should be troubled because sin is flaunted in our wayward society. Evil is called good; good is called evil. Houses of God have become houses of men. Lying voices soothe itching ears. Souls are led astray. False teaching is circular in that it comes from hell and leads right back to hell. The dignity of human life is discarded. Chaos and blood mark our streets. Tragically, one of the most dangerous places to be in our society is in a human womb. Some of the dark alleys in our largest cities are not as dangerous. The news of the day is simply bad, day after day. We should be troubled!

In the midst of all this present trouble, consider this comforting truth: "But this I call to mind, and therefore I have hope: The steadfast love of the LORD never ceases; His mercies never come to an end; they are new every morning; great is Your faithfulness" (Lamentations 3:21–23). The present day overflows with the Lord's mercy for you. His well of mercy never runs dry. The Lord is your front and rear guard at all times. His love is unchanging. The days come and go, but the Lord is with us always. Each day begins and ends with His mercy. Morning, noon, and night, day by day, moment by moment, the Lord is with you.

We face challenges every day. Some days are easier than others. Some mornings we don't even want to get out of bed. If the day appears ominous and foreboding, how do we face it? How do we face the dark night when our troubles go unresolved or get even worse? By turning to the Lord, whose face shines upon us. Turn to the Lord in prayer, daily digest His Holy Word, remember your Baptism. Receive the gifts He gives in Word and Sacrament as often as you are able. There may be no lengthy strategies, no blueprint, and no bill from a life coach for you just to survive. What is certain is that the present day is a gift to you from the Lord. He will take care of you. We do not pray with timidity and trepidation. Rather, we pray boldly and with faith, "Give us this day our daily bread." Breathe deeply and know that His love and mercy are with you every moment of every single day. We err when we go through the day needlessly alone, without reading the Word or speaking to the Lord in prayer.

What lies ahead in the days to come? We do not know the intricate details of what the future holds, but more importantly, we know our loving Lord holds the tiniest matters and the biggest picture in His hands. Pressing the point, what lies ahead for all of us is death. Whether we are a king or a peasant, well-known or unknown, wealthy or destitute, we only have so many heartbeats and breaths on this side of eternity. The math is simple: one out of one dies. Death is the common denominator of us all. So be it. We also know what is ahead for us by God's grace, for the Lord has told us in His Holy Word the truth that we are God's baptized children and heirs of heaven. That makes our earthly pilgrimage one of comfort and peace. The compass needle of our lives does not point to the unknown but to the certain and true north that is the love of Christ and the place He has prepared for us. We are strangers and sojourners here; heaven is our home by grace.

That said, we all know someone who is so terrified of death that they fail to embrace earthly life. Such fear paralyzes, squeezes, and strangles the joy out of us. There is no need for that! Instead, cherish the truth that death is a defeated enemy. The empty tomb of Christ fills us with enduring comfort. The final say does not belong to death, but to Christ, and He says, never to be silenced, "I go and prepare a place for you, I will come again and will take you to Myself, that where I am you may be also" (John 14:3). The obituary of death is written, never to be amended. Death is gagged, bound, and defeated. Death is dead. Your name is written by grace in the Lamb's Book of Life. It is written in His precious blood, indelible and eternal.

Some in this world would have you wonder about Judgment Day and what will come at the end of the world. You, child of God, have nothing to fear. The One who had the say in the beginning has the say at the end. You are the Lord's little lamb, and He is your loving Shepherd. His rod and His staff are comforts to you. He is your Good Shepherd who knows you, and you know Him (see John 10:1–21). "Come," Christ will say on the Last Day. "You have inherited the kingdom I prepared for you." He laid down His life for us and stands before the Father for us. Our sins are not enumerated before our Creator. They are sent away as far as the east is from the west. We pray, "Come, Lord Jesus" in faith, not in fear, for His perfect love casts out fear. The One who loves you controls all history, from beginning to end. His sovereignty is supreme.

TREASURE: Recall the beginning of this chapter, when I asked you to think about your past, present, and future. Entrust your life to your Good Shepherd. For now and for all eternity, you have Christ. More important, He has you! He will never forget you. He loved you before the world was created. He loves you today and will love you on the Last Day. And He will love you through eternity. His love has no end. Join David and joyously say, "My times are in Your hand" (Psalm 31:15). There is no better place than those pierced, living, and loving hands, for they hold your past, present, and future most lovingly.

Take Heart

An Assured Past, Present, and Future

Jesus Christ is the same yesterday and today and forever. (Hebrews 13:8)

Do not boast about tomorrow, for you do not know what a day may bring. (Proverbs 27:1)

And which of you by being anxious can add a single hour to his span of life? (Matthew 6:27)

In peace I will both lie down and sleep; for You alone, O Lord, make me dwell in safety. (Psalm 4:8)

Blessed be the Lord, who daily bears us up; God is our salvation. (Psalm 68:19)

Prayer

Loving Savior, thank You for holding me in Your most gracious and loving hands. You have loved me from all eternity, and Your love has no end. My past, present, and future are forever in Your hands of mercy and grace. Comfort me and be with me always, even unto the close of the age. One thing never changes, and that is Your love for me. In Your name. Amen.

CHAPTER 18

Assurance

MY TROUBLE: Fear(s)

HIS TREASURE: Assurance

TROUBLE: Think about a time when you felt intense fear. Your heart pounded, and your mind raced with dark, careening thoughts. Your hands trembled, and beads of sweat formed on your brow. You had no control. You thought, *This could be it.* How would you complete these statements: I am afraid of ________. I am afraid that______. I am afraid when________.

Such was the situation Jesus' disciples experienced one night on the Sea of Galilee. They had gone on toward Capernaum while Jesus went out alone to pray. Then suddenly everything changed. The once-calm sea became tempestuous. The gentle wind was now increasingly fierce. Waves once small became menacing, tossing the boat up and down. Stout hearts beating within the chests of the disciples raced with fear. Muscles ached as they tried to steer the vessel from out in the open in the middle of the lake toward the shelter of the shore. Faces were pelted with rain. Dark thoughts raced through minds, capsizing and drowning in the murky depths among the men. This was not the smooth sailing they had set out in!

A figure walking on the waves came into view during the fourth watch of the night. "A ghost!" they screamed in fear.

No, this was not a ghost. It was the Son of God in the flesh. Immediately, He spoke to the terrified men: "Take heart; it is I. Do not be afraid" (Matthew 14:27). You know what happened next. Impetuous Peter tried to walk on the water the same way Jesus did. He couldn't, of course, for he was not fully focused on Jesus. Jesus reached out to save Peter, got into the boat with the others to save them, and calmed the storm.

Take heart; it is Jesus. The Lord is with you at all times, during every watch of your life. Storms come, and fears rise like large waves crashing upon the hull of our hearts. We are weak; He is strong. Our words are powerless; His Word is efficacious. We feel like we are rowing in the middle of a storm far from shore. The Lord is not far from you. He is with you. He speaks to comfort and calm you. Let us not be afraid to speak of fear! Let us all the more boldly speak of the gift of assurance from the voice of Christ.

Phobias can be listed from A to Z. There is a phobia for every letter of the alphabet. Some are easily deciphered. Acoustiaphobia is the fear of loud noises. Zoophobia is the fear of animals. Hemophobia is the fear of blood. Hydrophobia is the fear of water. Others, I fear, are more obscure. Hippopotomonstrosesquippedaliophobia is the fear of long words. Koumpounophobia is the fear of clothes buttons. Ombrophobia is the fear of rain. Arachibutyrophobia is the fear of getting peanut butter stuck on the roof of your mouth. Atelophobia is the fear of not knowing.

We are all afraid at times. "They were terrified," we read concerning the disciples on the stormy sea (Matthew 14:26). David wrote, after being captured by the Philistines, "When I am afraid, I put my trust in You" (Psalm 56:3). We can be afraid standing on dry land and even safely within the confines of our own homes. At any age, at any time, at any place, fear can arise. Our lives are calm one minute, then chaotic the next.

How would you answer the following question: "What are you afraid of?" (Please do not say *nothing;* I fear that would be a lie.) We all have fears, including the following examples:

The phone rings, and we are afraid something tragic has happened to someone we love.

Our children go to college, and we are afraid they will fall away from the Lord.

We age and fear we will end up in a nursing home.

An argument takes place, and we fear our family is fractured forever.

The stock market plunges, and we are afraid of a financial free fall.

A friend seems cold, and we fear the friendship is over.

A slowdown hits the economy, and we fear for our employment.

Our spouse is distant, and we fear for our marriage.

We fear going to the doctor for test results.

We are afraid to board an airplane after planning a trip.

We fear our sins are too great to be forgiven, that the Lord will abandon us, that no one cares, and that we are all alone. We are afraid to live and afraid to die. Fear paralyzes us, freezing us in place.

We have many fears. I could enumerate all of mine, and many pages would follow. You too? What are we to do? Despair as if there is no hope? Remain petrified in a state of fear and do nothing? Tremble in the dark? Lock the doors and windows?

Are our fears so large and the Lord so small? Are our fears so powerful and the Lord so weak? Is there no one to calm, steady, and assure us?

There is. Christ. He stills your trembling heart with His Word. My fearful friend, listen to what the Lord says to you: "Fear not, for I am with you; be not dismayed, for I am your God; I will strengthen you, I will help you, I will uphold you with My righteous right hand" (Isaiah 41:10). Fearful one, He says to you, "Peace I leave with you; My peace I give to you. Not as the world gives do I give to you. Let not your heart be troubled, neither let them be afraid" (John 14:27). He speaks, and it is done. He speaks, and the gift is given.

In the account in Matthew, the One who allowed the storm to rock the disciples' boat also steered their vessel safely into the harbor. Like the disciples, we can cast our raging fears upon Jesus. We learn from our fears to turn to Christ, our rock of refuge, our staff and shelter always. He holds us by the hand and will never release His grip of grace; He will never leave us in the dreadful darkness of fear. Even in a raging storm, we can say, "I sought the LORD, and He answered me and delivered me from all my fears" (Psalm 34:4). In our storm-tossed life, we can say, "When the cares of my heart are many, Your consolations cheer my soul" (Psalm 94:19). On the darkest days, "The LORD is my light and my salvation; whom shall I fear? The LORD is the stronghold of my life; of whom shall I be afraid?" (Psalm 27:1). On the longest night, we can remember, "God is not man, that He should lie, or a son of man, that He should change His mind. Has He said, and He will not do it? Or has He spoken, and He will not full it?" (Numbers 23:19).

TREASURE: Think back to the beginning of this chapter and the list of names of fears. Do you know what taphophobia is? It is the fear of being buried alive. Have you heard of myrmecophobia? It is the fear of ants. What about erythrophobia? It is the fear of blushing.

Here is the most important question: Do you know that at all times you can cast your every fear—whether that fear is massive or minuscule—on Christ, your Lord? Yes, you do! He tells you the same thing He told the disciples: "Take heart; it is I."

Take Heart

Assurance

I sought the LORD, and He answered me and delivered me from all my fears. (Psalm 34:4)

When I am afraid, I put my trust in You. (Psalm 56:3)

And behold, I am with you always, to the end of the age. (Matthew 28:20)

Say to those who have an anxious heart, "Be strong; fear not! Behold, your God will come with vengeance, with the recompense of God. He will come and save you." (Isaiah 35:4)

For I, the LORD your God, hold your right hand; it is I who say to you, "Fear not, I am the one who helps you." (Isaiah 41:13)

But immediately Jesus spoke to them, saying, "Take heart; it is I. Do not be afraid." (Matthew 14:27)

Prayer

Lord Jesus, ever compassionate and loving Savior, whenever I am afraid, I turn to You for comfort and calm, for peace and protection. My heart is storm-tossed, and waves of fear crash upon me. By faith, given to me by the Holy Spirit, through Your Word, and in the Holy Sacrament You instituted, I know that You quiet and still my fears. You are my staff and shield at all times. May I be still and know that You are God, my rock and my redeemer, my refuge and my shelter in every storm. Amen.

CHAPTER 19

Life Lessons

MY TROUBLE: Aging

HIS TREASURE: Life Lessons

TROUBLE: Clara was nearly one hundred years old. She still lived in her own home, and not a speck of dust was to be found anywhere. She served coffee and homemade rolls when I visited her. The changes she had witnessed and spoke of in her lifetime astounded me—from outhouses to indoor plumbing, from candles to electricity, from the Model T to luxury SUVs, from the rotary telephone to smartphones, from using horses in the field to remote-controlled tractors, and more. She was a wealth of knowledge and a joy to visit. Yet the years were taking a toll. Her vision was no longer 20-20. Her hearing wasn't as sharp. Her knees ached. And she admitted that she couldn't get as much done as she once had. "Getting old isn't easy," she said.

Think about your attitude toward aging. You may be like some people who embrace the advance of years, or you may be like others who dread it. Gray hair may be an embarrassment, so you cover it with dye. You may want to keep your smooth, young-looking complexion, so you use a popular cosmetic to keep it. Vitamins and supplements promise restored energy and cognition. Television infomercials, ads in magazines, promotions on social media lure you in with promises of a youthful appearance. You may even compare yourself to people you know. "Is my friend really seventy years old? She looks great; what does she use on her face?" "My neighbor always has energy, as if he has found that fountain of youth! Does he take vitamins?" "At this rate, they will look great and be going strong into their eighties and nineties!" We chase the mythical fountain of youth, when we have the font of every blessing in Christ.

There is nothing wrong with getting older. Aging is not a bane—it is a blessing. Our worth is not established by a number, nor is the quality of life. Why should we be embarrassed by our calloused hands and wrinkled brow? Why should we apologize for the days, months, years, and experiences the Lord has given us?

Think of the countless breaths and heartbeats the Lord has given you. Rather than fretting about getting older, embrace the undeniable fact. I, too, have looked in the mirror and thought, *What is happening to me?* I look through photographs spanning decades, and I see the physical changes the years have brought upon me. Aging certainly brings aches, pains, and challenges in many forms, but the accrued blessings outweigh any negatives. Those pictures of long ago—those were good times with loved ones that the Lord gave me, and I wouldn't change a thing! Would you?

Aging is presented in Holy Scripture as a positive. Consider these passages:

> **Grandchildren are the crown of the aged, and the glory of children is their fathers. (Proverbs 17:6)**
>
> **The glory of young men is their strength, but the splendor of old men is their gray hair. (Proverbs 20:29)**
>
> **Wisdom is with the aged, and understanding in length of days. (Job 12:12)**
>
> **So teach us to number our days that we may get a heart of wisdom. (Psalm 90:12)**

Aging is also presented as a negative:

> **Remember also your Creator in the days of your youth, before the evil days come and the years draw near of which you will say, "I have no pleasure in them." (Ecclesiastes 12:1)**

Aching joints, worsening eyesight, slower steps are the reality of aging and the challenges that come with it, but the positives of longevity far outweigh the negatives. You are older now than you were when you first started reading this paragraph. Thanks be to God for those extra heartbeats and breaths He so graciously gives us.

Psalm 71 fits in beautifully here. At the dawn of life: "For you, O Lord, are my hope, my trust, O LORD, from my youth. Upon You I have leaned from before my birth; You are He who took me from my mother's womb. My praise is continually of You" (vv. 5–6). Through life: "With the mighty deeds of the Lord God I will come; I will remind them of Your righteousness, Yours alone" (v. 16). Then the days of old age: "O God, from my youth You have taught me, and I still proclaim Your wondrous deeds. So even to old age and gray hairs, O God, do not forsake me" (vv. 17–18).

Valuable life lessons are learned from the aged. The older people in our lives are a rich resource when we take the time to listen and learn from them. They teach us valuable lessons in appreciating what we have, the reward of hard work, the gift of spending time with family. Stories about your personal family history give context to your life today and teach that life really is short and time passes quickly. There's wisdom to glean from personal experience, and it's ripe for the picking. Job stated, "Wisdom is with the aged" (Job 12:12).

The Lord has allotted a certain number of days for your life. Each day is His gift to you! Approaching each day with this attitude means that you can be young at age 90. Or the opposite can be true, and a person may feel old at age 25. Perspective makes all the difference. Our every moment is held lovingly in the Lord's hands. The important point is not the numerical years of our life but the life in those years. Let us see each day as a precious gift from the Lord! Think of the gift of days, the accrued blessings, someone in their eighties or nineties has received.

Take a good look in the mirror. (Perhaps you first need to get your glasses to see better; that is okay!) Now, look at your reflection. Whether you see gray hair, crow's feet, bags under your eyes, or sunspots, you are beautiful. How blessed you are!

TREASURE: Recall Clara, the one-hundred-year-old I introduced at the beginning of this chapter. Going through her photo album with her took hours, but it was a joy. She spoke appreciatively of seeing her children's children's children's children! "Getting old isn't easy, but it certainly is a blessing," Clara said.

Blessing after blessing was captured in those black-and-white (and then, color) photographs. Each caused her to recall and rejoice in moments and times and people the Lord had given her through all the years. Although her eyesight was not good, she clearly saw God's loving hand in her life. She readily gave thanks for the copious blessings given to her as an infant at the font and as she neared her one hundredth birthday. She had an amazing perspective. To listen to her was to glean wisdom. The fitting word *blessing* was often spoken from her own lips.

"My back is starting to ache," she said the last time I was there. "I think I will take a nap now, Pastor. Please, take the sweet rolls with you."

I did take the pastries, and so much more. Thank you, Clara!

Oh, that we all would listen to and learn from those older than us. For these dear ones are a treasure.

Take Heart

Life Lessons

Wisdom is with the aged, and understanding in length of days. (Job 12:12)

Do not cast me off in the time of old age; forsake me not when my strength is spent. (Psalm 71:9)

You shall stand up before the gray head and honor the face of an old man, and you shall fear your God: I am the LORD. (Leviticus 19:32)

So teach us to number our days that we may get a heart of wisdom. (Psalm 90:12)

Listen to your father who gave you life, and do not despise your mother when she is old. (Proverbs 23:22)

Prayer

Heavenly Father, each day is a gift from You, replete with Your blessings. Every breath and heartbeat I take is Your gift. Thank You for the people in my life that You have used to mold and shape me in the Christian faith. I thank You for their wisdom and their witness to You. May I honor the aged and the wisdom they hold. Teach me to number my days, each one as a gift and a blessing so that I do not waste the time You have allotted me. In Jesus' name. Amen.

CHAPTER 20

A Clean Heart

MY TROUBLE: Lust and Pornography

HIS TREASURE : A Clean Heart

TROUBLE: As supper was simmering on the stove, a woman sat in her living room for a few minutes to rest her feet. Her husband was in the kitchen at the counter, handling some work on his computer. The aroma of roast beef wafted through the house. The table was set, and a nice supper awaited them. They always sat at the table and conversed, even though their children were long gone from their home. She rose to make the gravy and glanced appreciatively in her husband's direction. Such a hard worker. How she loved him! The atmosphere was instantly shattered when she caught a glimpse of the computer screen. She could hardly believe her eyes! Foul and filthy images came into focus. Her husband was watching porn.

"Sin is crouching at the door. Its desire is contrary to you, but you must rule over it," the Lord warned Cain at his seething anger over his own brother, Abel (Genesis 4:7). Sin would master Cain, and he would murder his brother. Sin is crouching at your door and mine, and with the help of God, we must master it—not excuse it—by confessing it and repenting of it.

Pornography is endemic. The days of sneaking into some seedy theater to view pornography have long since passed. Pornography is now a simple tap of the finger away on your computer or phone. Lewd images can be quickly and easily viewed in the convenience of your own living room. Technological advancement isn't the problem; how and why we use it is. Pornography is big business, and there is a big cost to be paid. "What is the big deal?" someone may ask. "No one is getting hurt." But the person who makes such a comment has been mastered.

It may be a surprise to learn that people can become addicted to pornography. Medical studies bear this out. Viewing such images changes the brain by altering neuro pathways. Over time, the brain is no longer as readily stimulated, and what was once thrilling becomes boring. The brain craves increased stimuli and increasingly graphic images.

Addiction is a frightening word. Pornography fosters guilt, shame, and sorrow. As with any addiction, a person affected may be in a cycle of vowing to never see it again. Then he or she seeks it all the more. Over and over. Pornography enslaves. And like other addicted people, a person may blame others instead of taking responsibility for his or her actions. "My wife ignored me, so I . . ." "My husband gained weight, so I looked at . . ." These are hollow, harmful excuses.

An additional harm is that pornography objectifies and demeans other human beings—not only those on the screen and in the photos, but also people in real life. Wives and husbands.

Sons and daughters. Viewing pornography communicates to one's spouse that he or she is not attractive enough or respected enough. The person viewing pornography says he or she does not care how his or her spouse feels. These are heartless, harmful messages.

Relationships are destroyed by pornography. It is injurious because it breaks hopes, hearts, and homes. Lust always tears down and destroys marriages and families.

Viewing pornography is utterly selfish behavior. The person engaged in viewing it indicates that his or her desires and needs are paramount to those of his or her spouse. The thrill of it leads to secret behavior, hiding, and lying—all of which are demeaning and damaging to relationships. One married man told me, "Watching porn is so much easier than dealing with a real flesh-and-blood relationship." His deeply wounded flesh-and-blood wife did not agree. Neither do I.

The excuse that "everyone does it" is untrue and foolish. (By the way, morality is not established by majority but by the Lord Himself.) Lust is sinful, self-centered, and self-serving. Lust greedily leaves a trail of broken relationships in its path, leaves a host of hurting people in its swirling wake.

Did you know these things about pornography? Maybe not. Now you do. The next question is, do you care? Be aware, for sin is crouching at your door!

It's possible that you have never seen porn, but you may have seen foul, filthy images in the theater of your own mind. The sins of lust, pride, and arrogance are crouching at your door.

Sadly, pornography has mastered you. Let what has been done in the dark now come into the light. Open wide the door. Make no more excuses, keep no more secrets—the time for honesty has come. Stop the cycle. Own your actions by confessing, "I am a porn addict. I have hurt my family, my spouse, my children, and myself. I have been selfish. Sin has had its way with me. Lord, forgive me. Help me resist the temptation."

All of heaven rejoices with those words. Repent. Be accountable. Seek forgiveness from those you have hurt. Keep the computer in a public space. Do not hide the phone. Replace the profane with the pure, the lies with truth. Resolve, one minute at a time, one hour at a time, one day at a time to resist the beast.

Know this: we all are weak and foolish, and we cannot resist temptation on our own. The evil one and our sinful flesh will test our resolve again and again. The foul images that have been seared into your mind will take you off guard. "Just once more, then I will quit," you reason. You cannot handle this by yourself.

Here is the point: you are not alone. You have those who love you, and above all, you have Christ, who loves you. He forgives you. He is with you. You can rejoice in His word of pardon, in His steady and sure love for you. The chains of sin fall away. The cell door is opened, flung off its hinges. The darkness is overcome in light. There is no need to walk back into the dark. There's no need to put on shame. You are wrapped in the garments of salvation. Jesus is your strength, mighty fortress, refuge, and rock. A new day has dawned for you. A new tomorrow as well. You now have a clean heart, created in you by the Lord. Drink deeply from the well of His grace and mercy and stand, forgiven one, in the light of His love.

TREASURE: Recall the scene at the beginning of this chapter. The woman was deeply hurt. "How could you do this to me?" Her husband had been reviewing his sermon on the computer when she left the room. Yes, he was a pastor. The wolf had sunk his teeth into an undershepherd of Christ. Who cares about supper now? The evening was ruined. And perhaps the marriage was too.

The man confessed his sin with repentant tears. He asked for forgiveness, promised to stop looking at lewd images, and looked to his wife for her mercy. But she was humiliated and couldn't stand to be in the same room with him. He had betrayed her trust and broken their marriage vows. Of course she forgave him. But his behavior was egregious. What was there for her to do but leave? She packed a suitcase and went to a motel.

After a legal separation, months of marriage counseling and individual counseling, the couple reconciled. It was the hardest thing either had ever done, but together, they worked to see each other through the breech. This couple knew that divorce was not part of God's plan. They knew they would have to be constantly forgiving of the other. They also knew that God's forgiveness would heal them both.

The husband sought an accountability partner in a brother pastor, who spoke to him the words of Holy Absolution. He thanked God this had come to light. He kept his promise to stop keeping secrets. He never looked at lewd images online again and invited his wife to review the history on his computer at will.

Their marriage was never the same. She was always on guard. He grew impatient with her lack of trust. But they recommitted to their vows to God and to each other. In time, with the help of God, they were able to draw close to each other and give thanks for the gift of their relationship.

Throughout their marriage, they were guided by this passage from Paul's letter to the Romans:

> **All have sinned and fall short of the glory of God, and are justified by His grace as a gift, through the redemption that is in Christ Jesus, whom God put forward as a propitiation by His blood, to be received by faith. This was to show God's righteousness, because in His divine forbearance He had passed over former sins. (Romans 3:23–25)**

Thankfully, a marriage and a ministry were saved. Praise be to God!

Take Heart

A Clean Heart

Do not be conformed to this world, but be transformed by the renewal of your mind, that by testing you may discern what the will of God, what is good and acceptable and perfect. (Romans 12:2)

I will give them a heart to know that I am the Lord, and they shall be My people and I will be their God, for they shall return to Me with their whole heart. (Jeremiah 24:7)

Create in me a clean heart, O God, and renew a right spirit within me. (Psalm 51:10)

Abstain from the passions of the flesh, which war against your soul. (1 Peter 2:11)

Flee from sexual immorality. Every other sin a person commits is outside the body, but the sexually immoral person sins against his own body. (1 Corinthians 6:18)

Whatever is true, whatever is honorable, whatever is just, whatever is pure, whatever is lovely, whatever is commendable, if there is any excellence, if there is anything worthy of praise, think about these things. (Philippians 4:8)

Prayer

Gracious and merciful Lord, I confess that my thoughts have been foul, filthy, and unfitting for a child of God. Jesus, light of the world, I have been living in the darkness of lust and lewdness. Sin has had its way with me. I have readily opened the door to sin.

Grant me a repentant heart. Forgive me. May I walk in the light of Your love. Thank You for Your mercy. I rejoice that You have mastered sin for me. Create in me a clean heart, O God, and renew a right spirit within me. In Jesus' name. Amen.

Epilogue

You are troubled. I am too.

Now what? Take heart! In your every trial, trouble, and tribulation, the treasure of Christ and His comforting love is there for you. "Peace be with you," the living and loving Savior says. The gift of His peace is yours.

You are comforted! I am too!

Others are troubled too. May their troubled state be a beacon for you, a summons to care, to reach out your hand, to speak words of scriptural encouragement, to listen, to pray, to bring comfort to them in Christ, your Good Shepherd and theirs. Christ carries each of us in His loving arms our whole lives through. His peace and love, comfort and mercy are bestowed upon us unfailingly each day.

Is life ever truly trouble free? Not on this side of heaven. Treasure this: we are truly and abundantly comforted by the Word of God for us, by the washing and regeneration of our Baptism, and by the sustaining Holy Meal.

Take heart, for Jesus promises, "My peace I give to you" (John 14:27).